PRO
EI

BOOK I

PROPERTIUS
ELEGIES

BOOK I

EDITED BY

W. A. CAMPS

formerly Master of Pembroke College

 CAMBRIDGE
UNIVERSITY PRESS

Published by the Press Syndicate of the University of Cambridge
The Pitt Building, Trumpington Street, Cambridge CB2 1RP
40 West 20th Street, New York, NY 10011-4211, USA
10 Stamford Road, Oakleigh, Melbourne 3166, Australia

ISBN 0 521 29210 7

First published 1961
Reprinted 1966, 1967, 1969, 1972
First paperback edition 1977
Reprinted 1981, 1985, 1988, 1990, 1992, 1995, 1999

Tranferred to digital printing 2001

PREFACE

The first book of Propertius' elegies is a convenient book for separate study. It appeared as a separate unit in the first place. It contains some of Propertius' best poetry. It represents a distinct and interesting phase of his poetical activity. It affords by itself sufficient evidence for the assessment of his place in the history of the Latin love elegy. It provides an instructive example of the way in which an Augustan 'book' was arranged. Moreover, it is comparatively free from major textual problems of the kind that arise all too often elsewhere in Propertius' works.

In making this edition I have referred constantly to the editions of Propertius' complete works by Paley (1872) and by Butler and Barber (1933); to Postgate's edition of some selected elegies (1884); to D. R. Shackleton Bailey's *Propertiana* (1956); and of course to P. J. Enk's big Latin-annotated edition (1946) of Book I itself. (My debt to Rothstein's admirable commentary (1920) is indirect, for I did not read it till my own was in all essentials complete.) The present work is not merely a compilation. But it could not have been produced at all without the help of the authors named above. Still less could it have been produced without the help of three Cambridge friends, Mr Sandbach, Mr Wilkinson and Mr Lee, who between them have removed so many errors and suggested so many improvements that this book, apart from its deficiencies, is by now almost as much theirs as mine. I am also deeply obliged to Professor Mynors, who read the draft at a later stage and gave me a great deal of help and criticism. It is a pleasant duty to thank all these for their kindness; and others also, whom I have not named here. Of course none of them can be held accountable for the mistakes that will be found in the final product, for obstinacy and afterthought have played their part as well.

Propertius is an author whose language is frequently unusual and frequently seems, or is, ambiguous; with the result that many passages in his works have been understood in a great number of different ways. Where it has seemed to me that no clear choice between alternatives was possible I have usually set out the alternatives and left the reader to exercise his own preference. Where however a particular interpretation has seemed to me definitely preferable to others, I have usually not mentioned or discussed alternatives, even though some may have been favoured by commentators whose authority demands respect. This procedure was necessary if the commentary was to be kept compact enough for the needs and the purse of the everyday reader. But it is of course arbitrary, and I hope that the reason given will be felt sufficient to excuse it.

For the same reason I have not attempted to identify in the notes the authors of the numerous interpretations and illustrations that I have adopted from friends or from previous commentators.

For information about the manuscripts and other matters relevant to the constitution of the text reference can conveniently be made to E. A. Barber's Oxford text (and introduction) of 1953, from which almost the whole of the sparing textual apparatus printed here has been excerpted, with the kind permission of the Delegates of the Clarendon Press. The text printed here differs from the Oxford text in a certain number of places; a list of these is provided on page 14 for the convenience of anyone who wishes to use the Oxford text in conjunction with the notes of this book.

W. A. C.

CAMBRIDGE

NOTE ON SECOND IMPRESSION

Some additions have been incorporated in the *apparatus criticus* and the commentary; a few which could not be incorporated appear separately on p. 102. In the text, the vulgate reading has been restored in xi, 5 and the MSS. reading in xvii, 11; and changes of punctuation have been made in i, 30 and xiii, 36. In the introduction small changes have been made on pp. 3 and 11, the former correcting a statement about Alexandrian love-poetry which was inaccurately phrased. I am grateful to the reviewers and friends whose criticisms suggested these amendments, and to the printers for making the amendments possible. There would have been more of them if practical considerations had allowed.

W. A. C.

CAMBRIDGE

CONTENTS

INTRODUCTION

Propertius' works

Propertius' works consist exclusively of poems in the elegiac metre. In the manuscripts they are divided into four books, containing respectively 22, 34, 25 and 11 elegies, making a total of 92. As, however, several of these are subdivided by modern editors, the total in modern editions is usually larger.

Most of the elegies in the first three books are on the subject of love. But there are some on other subjects. Several for instance, though outwardly attached to the love theme, are really concerned with Propertius' achievements and ambitions as a poet rather than with his feelings as a lover. In several again there is no pretence of a connexion with the love theme. Thus I, xxi is about the death of a kinsman of the poet in the Perusine war; I, xxii is about the poet's birthplace; III, xviii is a funeral elegy on the death of Augustus' heir Marcellus; III, xxii is an encomium on Italy; and so on.

Many, though not all, of the elegies that are concerned with love refer specifically to the feelings of Propertius for a mistress whom he calls Cynthia. This subject completely dominates the first book and is still prominent in the second; in the third book it falls into the background, and the last two elegies of that book (which are not necessarily the last in order of composition) declare the relationship at an end. Cynthia is actually *named* in 13 elegies out of 22 in the first book, in 12 out of 34 in the second book, and in 3 out of 25 in the third book. Of the love elegies that do not name Cynthia some certainly refer to her (e.g. I, ii and I, vii); some certainly refer to other women (e.g. II, xxii); and some again are general essays on topics arising from the love theme, such as II, xii in which the poet discusses the reasons why love is appropriately represented with wings, or III, xix in which he argues, with illustrations from mythology, that the passions of women are more violent than those of men.

Book IV in its atmosphere and character stands apart from the rest. Of the 11 elegies that compose it, five (or six if we count the elegy that serves as introduction to the whole book) are 'aetiological' poems, i.e. describe the origin in legend or history of some place-name or religious institution or the like. Of the remainder, three are related indeed to the love theme but in a manner that contrasts sharply with that of the previous books. Of these IV, v represents a bawd giving advice to a younger woman on the exploitation of lovers; IV, vii recounts the appearance of Cynthia to Propertius in a dream on a night after her funeral; IV, viii shows Propertius caught by Cynthia in the company of a pair of less elegant courtesans. All are coloured strongly with an unromantic realism that is startlingly different from the emotional tone of the earlier books.

Hellenistic and rhetorical influences

In the form of a number of the elegies certain genres of Hellen-istic poetry are clearly recognizable. Thus I, xx is a brief narrative of the Hylas story addressed to a friend of the poet: it repeats the form of Theocritus XIII. In I, xxi the speaker asks a passer-by to carry the news of his death to his family: this is an adaptation of the form of epigrams such as that of Calli-machus in *A.P.* VII, dxxi. In III, iii the poet professes to have been advised by Apollo how to use his poetic gifts: this is an adaptation of a well-known passage from Callimachus' *Aitia*. In Book IV the same poem of Callimachus has given the idea for the five 'aetiological' poems (ii, iv, vi, ix, x).

Other elegies again seem in their form to show affinity with various types of composition that were practised at Rome as part of a young man's education. For instance, II, xii in which the poet discusses the representation of Love as a winged creature recalls an exercise mentioned later by Quintilian (II, iv, 26): *quid ita crederetur Cupido puer...et sagittis ac face armatus.* The praise of Spartan customs in III, xiv and the praise of Italy in III, xxii belong to the same class as the *laus legum* and *laus locorum* of Quintilian II, iv, 33 and III, vii, 27. The sermon in III, xiii is a *locus communis (in luxuriam)* such as those discussed by Quintilian II, iv, 22–3. The imaginary letter from wife to absent husband in IV, iii is a speech in character of the kind called a *prosopopoeia* by the teachers of rhetoric. It is not suggested that elegies such as these are no more than exercises; but it does appear likely that exercises such as those referred to have had some influence on their form.

The love elegy a creation of the Augustans

But the typical elegy on the love theme as we meet it in Propertius and his contemporary Tibullus and his successor Ovid—a piece of some extent in which the poet discourses about his own love (occasionally a friend's) or some occasion arising from it—seems to be a product of the Augustan age (if one may use the term loosely to embrace the whole period 43 B.C.–A.D. 14) and to have had no established form as predecessor in Greek or Latin literature. The known love poems of the Alexandrian elegists are epigrams in which the poet speaks of his own love in the compass of a few lines, or are narrative elegies in which the poet recounts or enumerates the love stories of mythology. The love poetry of Catullus belongs in *form* to the category of epigram. Both Quintilian in his review of Latin literature (*Inst. Or.* x) and Ovid when speaking of his predecessors in elegy (*Trist.* IV, x) agree in listing before Ovid three poets only: Gallus, Tibullus and Propertius. The first of these is Cornelius Gallus, subject of Virgil's tenth Eclogue, who incurred Augustus' displeasure as prefect of Egypt and committed suicide in 27 or 26 B.C. The Servian commentary on the tenth Eclogue says that Gallus *amorum suorum de Cytheride scripsit libros quattuor.* We may suppose,

3

though we do not know for certain, that these poems were elegies. Only one line of Gallus' making (a pentameter: *uno tellures diuidit amne duas*) has survived. We do not know at all how much of his output consisted of love elegies. But in view of the statements of Ovid and Quintilian it is presumably to him that the credit for inventing the genre[1] must go. We may think of it, if we wish to speculate, as an expansion of the epigram under the influence of that facility in the development of an idea (*copia*) which contemporary education sought to promote.

Its treatment by the Augustan elegists

The genre is handled by Propertius, Tibullus and Ovid in quite separate and distinctive ways. Ovid for instance makes it plain at the outset of his *Amores* that his feelings are not involved, and the whole collection proves to be a set of studies, by an extraordinarily inventive and articulate talent, on topics borrowed from existing love poetry—borrowed, of course, intentionally, and inviting reminiscence of previous treatments as part of the artistic effect at which the writer aims. In Tibullus and Propertius erotic feeling is an important factor, and in Propertius this feeling is unmistakably intense. But in them too we are conscious of a considerable inherited or conventional element, the exact extent of which we are not able to estimate. This point has to be kept in mind in interpreting any individual poem, which cannot always be safely understood as referring to a real occasion, even when it very definitely professes to do so. Another point that has to be kept in mind is the social context in which the 'love affairs' of these poets purport to occur; this is different from the context of most English love poetry, and the reader has to be careful not to

---

[1] Catullus LXXVI by its length (26 lines) exceeds the limits of the epigram and bears a manifest resemblance to the love elegy of the Augustans. Cat. LXVIII is longer still, and foreshadows Propertius in its blending of mythology with personal statement. But these poems in Catullus appear as isolated experiments, not yet representative of an established genre.

assume a background of sentiment to these poems which belongs to another world than theirs.[1] For instance, lifelong devotion is often professed, but it is hardly conceivable (and this the participants know very well) that it can be realized in fact. The women concerned, who may be both highly accomplished and sincerely loved, are none the less professional courtesans, and their social category is separated from that of the men in the story by law as well as by custom.

Propertius' life

Very little is known of Propertius' life beyond what he tells us himself in his works. His name was Sextus Propertius, for he is so called by Donatus in his life of Virgil, in a passage almost certainly derived verbatim from Suetonius. He was an Umbrian, probably from the neighbourhood of Assisi (I, xxii and IV, i, 120 ff.). It can be assumed with some confidence that he was born not earlier than 57 B.C., since from IV, i, 120 ff. it appears that when he assumed the *toga uirilis* he had already forfeited most of his patrimony in the confiscations of 41–40 B.C., and an age of seventeen or more on assuming the *toga uirilis* would be unusual.[2] He lost his father in boyhood (IV, i, 120 ff.) and his mother in early manhood (IV, i, 120 ff. and II, xx, 15). While still very young he chose poetry instead of oratory for his career (IV, i, 120 ff.).

Not later than 30 B.C. (I, vi) he was captivated by Cynthia, the subject of so many of his poems, whose real name according

---

[1] Some idea of the social context, and of the variety of situations and of sentiment that might occur in it, may be got from the following: Terence, *Andria* 70–99 and *Eunuchus* 1–200 (where one must make due allowance for the difference of date and for the Greek background); Catullus X and XLV; Horace, *Epodes* xi and *Odes* I, xxv, III, xiv and IV, xiii; Propertius II, xxiii and IV, viii; Ovid, *Ars Amatoria, passim.* The list might of course be much longer.

It must be emphasized that Catullus' Lesbia and the elegist Sulpicia belong to a different category altogether.

[2] On the age for taking the *toga uirilis* see F. H. Sandbach in *Classical Review* (1940), p. 73.

to Apuleius (*Apologia* 10) was Hostia. She was a *meretrix*, as appears from poems such as II, vi where he compares her to famous courtesans like Lais, Thais and Phryne, or II, xvi where he says of her that *semper amatorum ponderat una sinus*, or I, iv where she is one of a class designated as *puellae* and her vexation at the loss of a lover is spoken of as a recurrent event. The affair, according to III, xxv, 3, lasted five years; but the figure five in the poem quoted may be a rough one, and the breach there recorded may not after all have been final. In IV, vii Cynthia has recently died.

At some point Propertius' younger contemporary Ovid (born 43 B.C.) entered his circle; for Ovid (*Trist.* IV, x, 45 ff.) claims often to have heard Propertius recite his love poems (*ignes*) and to have been associated with him in some kind of *sodalitium*; this can hardly have begun earlier than 26 B.C. when Ovid would be seventeen years old, and may not have begun till considerably later. At some time also Propertius seems to have married—unless he adopted an heir; for the younger Pliny (*Ep.* IX, xxii, 1) speaks of one Passennus Paullus as descended from him. He died not later than A.D. 2, since Ovid in the *Remedia Amoris* (763) speaks of him in that year in the past tense. The last datable reference in his extant works is to an event of 16 B.C. (see below).

Datable occasions in his works

The occasions of a few of the elegies are definitely datable, and this gives us at least a rough chronology of Propertius' poetic activity. In book I the sixth elegy is on an occasion connected with the proconsulship of L. Volcacius Tullus in Asia in 30–29 B.C. In book III the eighteenth elegy is on the death of Marcellus in 23 B.C. In book IV the eleventh elegy is a funeral laudation of the sister of P. Cornelius Scipio, who died (as appears from lines 85–6 of the poem) in 16 B.C., the year of her brother's consulship. In book II there is no allusion that fixes a definite date but several that fix upper limits of date; thus in the tenth elegy Octavian is addressed as Augustus, implying a date in 27 B.C. or later; in the thirty-fourth Cornelius Gallus is said (line 91) to have died 'lately', implying a date in 27–26 B.C. or not much later. In general therefore we can associate the four books with the years 30, 26, 23 and 16 B.C. respectively, it being understood of course that the composition of the poems in any one book may have been spread over several years. It is better not to speculate about dates of 'publication' since the conditions of publication in the ancient world were so different from those today that the term is likely to mislead.

The terms of IV, i, 131 do not naturally suggest that Propertius' assumption of the *toga uirilis* followed without any appreciable interval on the confiscations of 41–40 B.C. On the other hand the reader of Book I will probably form the impression that the author was fully adult; and when Propertius in I, xxii refers to the memory of his kinsman's death in the Perusine war of 40 B.C. as a great grief to himself personally it does not seem likely that he is referring to something that happened when he was twelve years old or less. These considerations may lead us to set the date of his birth later than 57, but earlier than 52 B.C. But it remains a matter of conjecture. All we really can assume with any confidence is that he was born in the decade beginning 57 B.C.

Character of Book I

Book I seems to have been in circulation in the ancient world as a separate volume, beside and apart from any collection of Propertius' works as a whole; for the gift that is the subject of Martial XIV, clxxxix is described as *Cynthia, iucundi carmen iuuenale Properti* under the heading *Monobiblos Properti*. And indeed of the 22 elegies that the book contains the first 19 are, or appear to be, all concerned with the Cynthia story and Cynthia is actually named in as many as 13 of them. The last three poems of the book are miscellaneous; xx is an elegiac narrative of the Hylas myth, xxi commemorates the death of a relative of the poet, and xxii identifies the region of his birth-place. The first and last poems of the book are both addressed to a friend named Tullus, who is also the addressee of vi and xiv.

Motives shared with Tibullus and other poets

In the poems on the love theme there will be found a number of characters, situations and motives that are found also in contemporary or earlier poets. For example the witch (cf. Tib. I, ii, 41), the rich rival (Tib. I, v, 47), the derisive friend (Tib. I, ii, 87), the friends who try to bring the infatuated man to his senses (Hor. *Epod.* XI, 25). Or again the moonlight shining through the window on the sleeping girl (Philodemus in *A.P.* v, cxxiii), the poet made witness of a friend's amour (Cat. XLV), the departure of the lady on an arduous journey with another lover   rg. *Ecl.* x), the lover uttering his complaint amid romantic scenery (Virg. *Ecl.* x), the lover outside the lady's closed door (Callimachus in *A.P.* v, xxiii and Tib. I, i, 56). Or again the contrast between the lover and the man of action (Tib. I, i, 53), the worthlessness of riches by comparison with love (Tib. I, ii, 75), the value of poetry as an instrument of love (Tib. II, iv, 15), the role of instructor or expert in love (Tib. I, iv, 9ff.); the loved one's protestations proved false (Tib. I, ix, 1), the arts of adornment used by women and reflections thereupon (Tib. I, viii, 9).

The number of coincidences here between Propertius and his slightly older contemporary Tibullus needs explanation. It is not of course likely that one is consistently echoing the other, for why, of two contemporaries, should we suppose one so original and one so suggestible? Moreover a number of the motives that are common to the two poets are observable in earlier literature, especially in comedy, in epigram and in Alexandrian narrative elegy. We seem to be dealing with a set of motives that are already established as it were as a convention. But how and when did such a convention become established? And what contribution to it was made by Gallus? We do not know. But we can conjecture that two factors were probably important. First, the collection of motives from past literature and adaptation of them to adorn a theme was a habit encouraged by contemporary education. Secondly, we can be sure that the poets of that time wrote far more than they ever made fully public, and that much of this was communicated by private recitation within literary coteries such as those of which we are aware in connexion with the early life of Virgil and Ovid.

Mythological allusion

A characteristically Propertian feature of these poems is the abundance of mythological allusion. This habit was favoured by the rhetoricians' method, taught at school, of enumerating examples to support an argument. It was favoured also by the example of the Hellenistic poets, who were fond of assembling and reciting legends that had some common element (loves of gods, loves of poets, unhappy loves, etc.); indeed, a Greek named Parthenius had compiled for Gallus a book[1] (in prose) of tales of unhappy love expressly to be used as a source of allusions in his own poetry. In Propertius the resulting allusions have a far from mechanical quality, and in passages such as I, iii, 1–8, or I, xix, 7–18, or II, xxviii, 49–58 it is plain that in his imagination the legends and their characters are alive. The notes on the mythology in the present volume are necessarily brief and jejune, and the reader who does not wish to lose the evocative value of the allusions is advised to look up in a dictionary of mythology those stories that he does not carry in his head.

[1] Called Ἐρωτικὰ παθήματα and still extant.

Arrangement of the contents of the book

The following list shows to whom Elegies i–xix are addressed:

  i Tullus

---

  ii Cynthia
 iii
 iv an interferer (Bassus)
  v an interferer (Gallus)

 vi Tullus

 vii Ponticus
viii Cynthia (with pendant viii B, to no named person)
 ix Ponticus

  x Gallus
 xi Cynthia (with pendant xii, to no named person)
xiii Gallus

xiv Tullus

 xv Cynthia
xvi
xvii soliloquy
xviii soliloquy

---

xix Cynthia

Elegy i (as also Elegy xxii) is addressed to Tullus in token that the book as a whole is as it were 'dedicated' to him. But its first word is 'Cynthia' and its natural counterpart in the collection is Elegy xix.

Elegies ii–xviii fall, as can be seen from the list above, into a series of groups,[1] and these groups are arranged within the

---

[1] Here is a comparison of Elegies ii–v and xv–xviii in respect of the percentage of pentameters in each that end in a word of more than two syllables: Elegy ii, 43·7%; Elegy iii, 60·9%; Elegy iv, 21·4%; Elegy v, 12·5%; Elegy xv, 66·6%; Elegy xvi, 75·0%; Elegy xvii, 21·4%; Elegy xviii, 25·0%.

book in chiastic order. A similarly chiastic order is found in
Ov. *Trist.* v (see Herrmann, cited by E. Martini, *Einleitung
zu Ovid* (1933), p. 52).

Elegies ii–xviii also fall into eight pairs, the members of
which are in some cases separated (ii and xv, iii and xvi, vi and
xiv, vii and ix, x and xiii, viii and xi), and sometimes juxta-
posed (iv and v, xvii and xviii). The members of each pair are
addressed to the same person, except where there is no person
addressed (iii and xvi, xvii and xviii), or there is an obvious
reason for departing from the principle (iv and v, where the
object is to exhibit two different types of interferer). The
members of each pair have always related subjects or situations
(e.g. ii and xv both reproach Cynthia for dressing herself up;
iii and xvi, which might at first sight seem to have nothing in
common, are in fact complementary to one another, pre-
senting in antithesis the complaints of neglected woman and
rejected man). And under the similarities that unite the
members of any pair there are always intentional differences
that contrast them.

Any reader interested in this aspect of Propertius' art will
be able to work out the subject further for himself. Enough
has been said here to show that the elegies of this book are not
biographical in the order of their arrangement, and only to a
limited extent biographical in character at all.

Quality of Propertius' poetry

A good deal has been said above about educational and literary
influences, conventions, formal arrangement and the like.
Some knowledge of these matters can prevent our making false
assumptions about the nature of Propertius' poetry and looking
for beauty in it in the wrong places. But it can tell us nothing
in a positive sense about the excellence or otherwise of the
poetry, any more than a knowledge of the subject of a picture
and the occasion for which it was commissioned and the style

of the school to which the artist belonged will tell one any-thing of the excellence or otherwise of the painting.

Propertius is a poet of a very high order; and he is so principally in virtue of three properties and (in his best passages) their exactly harmonious co-operation. The first of these is an abnormal sensitivity both of the senses and of the feelings—including incidentally the feeling evoked by proper names suggestive of distance, antiquity and legendary splen-dours. The second is a powerful pictorial imagination. The third is a strongly individual style, which can make glowing patterns of sound as it moves and which is, moreover, expressive in the utmost degree. These properties will be found abun-dantly illustrated in the poems of the present book: see for instance I, iii, 1–8, I, viii, 5–12, I, x, 1–10, I, xix, 1–12, I, xx, 33–49 and *passim*. Here are three examples taken from later books:

> nam neque Pyramidum sumptus ad sidera ducti,
>   nec Iouis Elei caelum imitata domus,
> nec Mausolei diues fortuna sepulcri
>   mortis ab extrema condicione uacant.
> aut illis flamma aut imber subducet honores,
>   annorum aut ictu, pondere uicta, ruent.
> at non ingenio quaesitum nomen ab aeuo
>   excidet: ingenio stat sine morte decus.
>
> (III, ii, 19–26)

> sunt aliquid manes: letum non omnia finit,
>   luridaque euictos effugit umbra rogos.
> Cynthia namque meo uisa est incumbere fulcro,
>   murmur ad extremae nuper humata uiae:
> cum mihi somnus ab exequiis penderet amoris,
>   et quererer lecti frigida regna mei.
> eosdem habuit secum quibus est elata capillos,
>   eosdem oculos: lateri uestis adusta fuit,
> et solitum digito beryllon adederat ignis,
>   summaque Lethaeus triuerat ora liquor.
> spirantisque animos et uocem misit: at illi
>   pollicibus fragiles increpuere manus.   (IV, vii, 1–12)

heu Veii ueteres! et uos tum regna fuistis,
 et uestro posita est aurea sella foro.
nunc intra muros pastoris bucina lenti
 cantat, et in uestris ossibus arua metunt.

(IV, x, 25–8)

Some useful sources of information

There is useful information about Propertius' metre and prosody in M. Platnauer's *Latin Elegiac Verse*[1] (Cambridge 1951); an excellent discussion of his use of language in the Introduction of J. P. Postgate's *Select Elegies of Propertius* (Macmillan 1884, often reprinted); and a lucid and comprehensive account of the history of love elegy in the Introduction of Butler and Barber's *Elegies of Propertius* (Oxford 1933). For longer works and for articles in periodicals reference must be made to the usual sources. The standard edition of Book I is now that of P. J. Enk (Leyden 1946, 2 vols.), the notes of which, in Latin, are both copious and valuable.

---

[1] Constructively reviewed by R. J. Getty in *Class. Phil.* XLVIII (1953), pp. 189–92.

VARIANTS FROM THE
OXFORD TEXT

The following readings in the text printed in this book differ from those of the Oxford text of 1957.

i, 24 Cytinaeis   30 *full-stop at end of line*
iii, 16 *no obeli*
iv, 14 dicere   24 *no commas*   27 nostri
v, 8 sciet
vii, 16 (quod nolim nostros, heu, uoluisse deos)
viii, 13 tali sub sidere   15 patiatur   19 utere *and semi-colon at end of line*   22 uera   26 Hylaeis
ix, 4 quaeuis
xi, 29 fuerunt
xii, 2 quod faciat nobis conscia Roma moram   9 num
xiii, 17 uerbis   35 qui tibi sit felix, quoniam nouus incidit, error
xv, 15–16 *stand after 22 instead of after 20*   21 elata
xvi, 8 exclusi   11–12 *no brackets*   38 †ingrato dicere pota loco†
xvii, 1 *comma at end of line*   11 reponere (*and so O.C.T. of 1960*)
xviii, 9 crimina   23–4 ...curas,...foribus?
xix, 14–16 *altered punctuation*   22 abstrahat, heu, nostro puluere iniquus amor
xx, 13 sint duri   50 fontibus
xxi, 5–7 seruato possint...me...Acca *and altered punctuation*
xxii, 5–8 *altered punctuation, and* sed *in line 6*

Also, in a few places amor *has been printed where the Oxford text has* Amor.

SIGLA

N = codex Neapolitanus, nunc Guelferbytanus Gudianus 224.
circa annum 1200 scriptus

A = codex Leidensis Vossianus Lat. 38 (desinit II, i, 63). circa
annum 1300 scriptus

F = codex Laurentianus plut. 36. 49. circa annum 1380 scriptus

P = codex Parisinus 7989. anno 1423 scriptus

D = codex Dauentriensis I. 82 (olim 1792) (incipit I, ii, 14).
saec. XV

V = codex Ottoboniano-Vaticanus 1514. saec. XV

Vo. = codex Leidensis Vossianus 117. saec. XV

O = codicum consensus $\begin{cases} NAFPVVo. & \text{ab initio ad I, ii, 13} \\ NAFPDVVo. & \text{a I, ii, 14} \end{cases}$

ς = codices deteriores

scito, lector, ex multis quae exstant codicum lectionibus et
virorum doctorum coniecturis paucas admodum in apparatu
ostendi.

SEXTI PROPERTI ELEGIARVM
LIBER PRIMVS

I

Cynthia prima suis miserum me cepit ocellis,
    contactum nullis ante cupidinibus.
tum mihi constantis deiecit lumina fastus
    et caput impositis pressit Amor pedibus,
donec me docuit castas odisse puellas   5
    improbus, et nullo uiuere consilio.
et mihi iam toto furor hic non deficit anno,
    cum tamen aduersos cogor habere deos.
Milanion nullos fugiendo, Tulle, labores
    saeuitiam durae contudit Iasidos.   10
nam modo Partheniis amens errabat in antris,
    ibat et hirsutas ille uidere feras;
ille etiam Hylaei percussus uulnere rami
    saucius Arcadiis rupibus ingemuit.
ergo uelocem potuit domuisse puellam: 15
    tantum in amore preces et bene facta ualent.
in me tardus Amor non ullas cogitat artis,
    nec meminit notas, ut prius, ire uias.
at uos, deductae quibus est fallacia lunae
    et labor in magicis sacra piare focis,   20
en agedum dominae mentem conuertite nostrae,
    et facite illa meo palleat ore magis!
tunc ego crediderim uobis et sidera et amnis
    posse Cytinaeis ducere carminibus.
et uos, qui sero lapsum reuocatis, amici,   25
    quaerite non sani pectoris auxilia.

post 11 *duo uu. excidisse putat Housman*   13 Hylaei *Franciscus Aretinus*: psilli O
16 preces O: fides *Fontein, Housman (cf. Tib.* III, iv, 64; vi, 46)
24 Cytinaeis *Hertzberg (qui etiam Cytaeines)*: cythalinis *et similia codd.*

fortiter et ferrum saeuos patiemur et ignis,
    sit modo libertas quae uelit ira loqui.
ferte per extremas gentis et ferte per undas,
    qua non ulla meum femina norit iter.   30
uos remanete, quibus facili deus annuit aure,
    sitis et in tuto semper amore pares.
in me nostra Venus noctes exercet amaras,
    et nullo uacuus tempore defit Amor.
hoc, moneo, uitate malum: sua quemque moretur   35
    cura, neque assueto mutet amore locum.
quod si quis monitis tardas aduerterit auris,
    heu referet quanto uerba dolore mea!

II

Quid iuuat ornato procedere, uita, capillo
    et tenuis Coa ueste mouere sinus,
aut quid Orontea crinis perfundere murra,
    teque peregrinis uendere muneribus,
naturaeque decus mercato perdere cultu,   5
    nec sinere in propriis membra nitere bonis?
crede mihi, non ulla tuae est medicina figurae:
    nudus Amor formae non amat artificem.
aspice quos summittat humus formosa colores,
    ut ueniant hederae sponte sua melius,   10
surgat et in solis formosius arbutus antris,
    et sciat indocilis currere lympha uias.
litora natiuis †persuadent† picta lapillis,
    et uolucres nulla dulcius arte canunt.
non sic Leucippis succendit Castora Phoebe,   15
    Pollucem cultu non Hilaira soror;

7 tu(a)e est *VVo.*: tua est *NAFP*   10 ut *edd.*: et *O*   13 persuadent
O: coniecerunt alii alia

non, Idae et cupido quondam discordia Phoebo,
  Eueni patriis filia litoribus;
nec Phrygium falso traxit candore maritum
  auecta externis Hippodamia rotis: 20
sed facies aderat nullis obnoxia gemmis,
  qualis Apelleis est color in tabulis.
non illis studium uulgo conquirere amantis:
  illis ampla satis forma pudicitia.
non ego nunc uereor ne sim tibi uilior istis: 25
  uni si qua placet, culta puella sat est;
cum tibi praesertim Phoebus sua carmina donet
  Aoniamque libens Calliopea lyram,
unica nec desit iucundis gratia uerbis,
  omnia quaeque Venus, quaeque Minerua probat. 30
his tu semper eris nostrae gratissima uitae,
  taedia dum miserae sint tibi luxuriae.

III

Qualis Thesea iacuit cedente carina
  languida desertis Cnosia litoribus;
qualis et accubuit primo Cepheia somno
  libera iam duris cotibus Andromede;
nec minus assiduis Edonis fessa choreis   5
  qualis in herboso concidit Apidano:
talis uisa mihi mollem spirare quietem
  Cynthia non certis nixa caput manibus,
ebria cum multo traherem uestigia Baccho,
  et quaterent sera nocte facem pueri.   10
hanc ego, nondum etiam sensus deperditus omnis,
  molliter impresso conor adire toro;
et quamuis duplici correptum ardore iuberent
  hac Amor hac Liber, durus uterque deus,

subiecto leuiter positam temptare lacerto   15
  osculaque admota sumere et arma manu,
non tamen ausus eram dominae turbare quietem,
  expertae metuens iurgia saeuitiae;
sed sic intentis haerebam fixus ocellis,
  Argus ut ignotis cornibus Inachidos.   20
et modo soluebam nostra de fronte corollas
  ponebamque tuis, Cynthia, temporibus;
et modo gaudebam lapsos formare capillos;
  nunc furtiua cauis poma dabam manibus;
omniaque ingrato largibar munera somno,   25
  munera de prono saepe uoluta sinu;
et quotiens raro duxti suspiria motu,
  obstupui uano credulus auspicio,
ne qua tibi insolitos portarent uisa timores,
  neue quis inuitam cogeret esse suam: 30
donec diuersas praecurrens luna fenestras,
  luna moraturis sedula luminibus,
compositos leuibus radiis patefecit ocellos.
  sic ait in molli fixa toro cubitum:
'tandem te nostro referens iniuria lecto   35
  alterius clausis expulit e foribus?
namque ubi longa meae consumpsti tempora noctis,
  languidus exactis, ei mihi, sideribus?
o utinam talis perducas, improbe, noctes,
  me miseram qualis semper habere iubes!   40
nam modo purpureo fallebam stamine somnum,
  rursus et Orpheae carmine, fessa, lyrae;
interdum leuiter mecum deserta querebar
  externo longas saepe in amore moras:
dum me iucundis lapsam sopor impulit alis.   45
  illa fuit lacrimis ultima cura meis.'

27 duxti ϛ: duxit O   45 lapsam *codd. plerique*: lassam P_2V_2

IV

Quid mihi tam multas laudando, Basse, puellas
    mutatum domina cogis abire mea?
quid me non pateris uitae quodcumque sequetur
    hoc magis assueto ducere seruitio?
tu licet Antiopae formam Nycteidos, et tu   5
    Spartanae referas laudibus Hermionae,
et quascumque tulit formosi temporis aetas;
    Cynthia non illas nomen habere sinat:
nedum, si leuibus fuerit collata figuris,
    inferior duro iudice turpis eat.   10
haec sed forma mei pars est extrema furoris;
    sunt maiora, quibus, Basse, perire iuuat:
ingenuus color et multis decus artibus, et quae
    gaudia sub tacita dicere ueste libet.
quo magis et nostros contendis soluere amores,   15
    hoc magis accepta fallit uterque fide.
non impune feres: sciet haec insana puella
    et tibi non tacitis uocibus hostis erit;
nec tibi me post haec committet Cynthia nec te
    quaeret; erit tanti criminis illa memor,   20
et te circum omnis alias irata puellas
    differet: heu nullo limine carus eris.
nullas illa suis contemnet fletibus aras,
    et quicumque sacer qualis ubique lapis.
non ullo grauius temptatur Cynthia damno   25
    quam sibi cum rapto cessat amore decus:
praecipue nostri. maneat sic semper, adoro,
    nec quicquam ex illa quod querar inueniam!

---

14 dicere *O*: ducere *ς*   16 accepta *O*: a(h) certa *Heinsius*   fallit uterque
NAFP: fallis utrumque *DV₁Vo*.   26 decus *Kraffert*: deus *O*

V

Inuide, tu tandem uoces compesce molestas
    et sine nos cursu, quo sumus, ire pares!
quid tibi uis, insane? meos sentire furores?
    infelix, properas ultima nosse mala,
et miser ignotos uestigia ferre per ignis,   5
    et bibere e tota toxica Thessalia.
non est illa uagis similis collata puellis:
    molliter irasci non sciet illa tibi.
quod si forte tuis non est contraria uotis,
    at tibi curarum milia quanta dabit!   10
non tibi iam somnos, non illa relinquet ocellos:
    illa feros animis alligat una uiros.
a, mea contemptus quotiens ad limina curres,
    cum tibi singultu fortia uerba cadent,
et tremulus maestis orietur fletibus horror,   15
    et timor informem ducet in ore notam,
et quaecumque uoles fugient tibi uerba querenti,
    nec poteris, qui sis aut ubi, nosse miser!
tum graue seruitium nostrae cogere puellae
    discere et exclusum quid sit abire domum;   20
nec iam pallorem totiens mirabere nostrum,
    aut cur sim toto corpore nullus ego.
nec tibi nobilitas poterit succurrere amanti:
    nescit amor priscis cedere imaginibus.
quod si parua tuae dederis uestigia culpae,   25
    quam cito de tanto nomine rumor eris!
non ego tum potero solacia ferre roganti,
    cum mihi nulla mei sit medicina mali;
sed pariter miseri socio cogemur amore
    alter in alterius mutua flere sinu.   30

8 sciet *ς*: solet *O*   9 tuis *N²*: ruis *O*   Votis *N²*: nostris *O*

quare, quid possit mea Cynthia, desine, Galle,
    quaerere: non impune illa rogata uenit.

VI

Non ego nunc Hadriae uereor mare noscere tecum,
    Tulle, neque Aegaeo ducere uela salo,
cum quo Rhipaeos possim conscendere montis
    ulteriusque domos uadere Memnonias;
sed me complexae remorantur uerba puellae,   5
    mutatoque graues saepe colore preces.
illa mihi totis argutat noctibus ignis,
    et queritur nullos esse relicta deos;
illa meam mihi iam se denegat, illa minatur,
    quae solet ingrato tristis amica uiro.   10
his ego non horam possum durare querelis:
    a pereat, si quis lentus amare potest!
an mihi sit tanti doctas cognoscere Athenas
    atque Asiae ueteres cernere diuitias,
ut mihi deducta faciat conuicia puppi   15
    Cynthia et insanis ora notet manibus,
osculaque opposito dicat sibi debita uento,
    et nihil infido durius esse uiro?
tu patrui meritas conare anteire securis,
    et uetera oblitis iura refer sociis.   20
nam tua non aetas umquam cessauit amori,
    semper at armatae cura fuit patriae;
et tibi non umquam nostros puer iste labores
    afferat et lacrimis omnia nota meis!
me sine, quem semper uoluit fortuna iacere,   25
    hanc animam extremae reddere nequitiae.

10 ingrato ς: irato O

multi longinquo periere in amore libenter, 27
  in quorum numero me quoque terra tegat. 28
non ego sum laudi, non natus idoneus armis: 29
  hanc me militiam fata subire uolunt. ——————— 30
at tu seu mollis qua tendit Ionia, seu qua
  Lydia Pactoli tingit arata liquor;
seu pedibus terras seu pontum carpere remis
  ibis, et accepti pars eris imperii:
tum tibi si qua mei ueniet non immemor hora, 35
  uiuere me duro sidere certus eris.

VII

Dum tibi Cadmeae dicuntur, Pontice, Thebae
  armaque fraternae tristia militiae,
atque, ita sim felix, primo contendis Homero,
  ₍sint modo fata tuis mollia carminibus:₎
nos, ut consuemus, nostros agitamus amores, 5
  atque aliquid duram quaerimus in dominam;
nec tantum ingenio quantum seruire dolori
  cogor et aetatis tempora dura queri.
hic mihi conteritur uitae modus, haec mea fama est,
  hinc cupio nomen carminis ire mei. 10
me laudent doctae solum placuisse puellae,
  Pontice, et iniustas saepe tulisse minas;
me legat assidue post haec neglectus amator,
  et prosint illi cognita nostra mala.
te quoque si certo puer hic concusserit arcu 15
  (quod nolim nostros, heu, uoluisse deos),
longe castra tibi, longe miser agmina septem
  flebis in aeterno surda iacere situ;
et frustra cupies mollem componere uersum,
  nec tibi subiciet carmina serus amor. 20

16 *ita scripsi*: quod nolim (*siue* nollim) nostros euiolasse deos O

24

tum me non humilem mirabere saepe poetam,
   tunc ego Romanis praeferar ingeniis;
nec poterunt iuuenes nostro reticere sepulcro
   'Ardoris nostri magne poeta, iaces.'
tu caue nostra tuo contemnas carmina fastu: 25
   saepe uenit magno faenore tardus amor.

VIIIA

Tune igitur demens, nec te mea cura moratur?
   an tibi sum gelida uilior Illyria?
et tibi iam tanti, quicumque est, iste uidetur,
   ut sine me uento quolibet ire uelis?
tune audire potes uesani murmura ponti   5
   fortis, et in dura naue iacere potes?
tu pedibus teneris positas fulcire pruinas,
   tu potes insolitas, Cynthia, ferre niues?
o utinam hibernae duplicentur tempora brumae,
   et sit iners tardis nauita Vergiliis,   10
nec tibi Tyrrhena soluatur funis harena,
   neue inimica meas eleuet aura preces!
atque ego non uideam tali sub sidere uentos,
   cum tibi prouectas auferet unda ratis,
ut me defixum uacua patiatur in ora   15
   crudelem infesta saepe uocare manu!
sed quocumque modo de me, periura, mereris,
   sit Galatea tuae non aliena uiae:
utere felici praeuecta Ceraunia remo;
   accipiat placidis Oricos aequoribus.   20
nam me non ullae poterunt corrumpere, de te
   quin ego, uita, tuo limine uera querar;

23-4 *post* 10 *Housman*   VIIIA   7 pruinas *DVVo.*: ruinas *NAFP*   13 sub
sidere *F₄V₂*: subsidere *O*   15-16 *post* 12 *Scaliger*   15 ut *Hemsterhuys*:
et *O*   19 utere *PDV₁Vo.*: ut te *NAFV₂*   22 uera *Passerat*: uerba *O*

nec me deficiet nautas rogitare citatos
   'Dicite, quo portu clausa puella mea est?',
et dicam 'Licet Atraciis considat in oris,   25
   et licet Hylaeis, illa futura mea est.'

VIIIb

Hic erit! hic iurata manet! rumpantur iniqui!
   uicimus: assiduas non tulit illa preces.
falsa licet cupidus deponat gaudia liuor:
   destitit ire nouas Cynthia nostra uias.   30
illi carus ego et per me carissima Roma
   dicitur, et sine me dulcia regna negat.
illa uel angusto mecum requiescere lecto
   et quocumque modo maluit esse mea,
quam sibi dotatae regnum uetus Hippodamiae,   35
   et quas Elis opes ante pararat equis.
quamuis magna daret, quamuis maiora daturus,
   non tamen illa meos fugit auara sinus.
hanc ego non auro, non Indis flectere conchis,
   sed potui blandi carminis obsequio.   40
sunt igitur Musae, neque amanti tardus Apollo,
   quis ego fretus amo: Cynthia rara mea est!
nunc mihi summa licet contingere sidera plantis:
   siue dies seu nox uenerit, illa mea est!
nec mihi riualis certos subducit amores: 45
   ista meam norit gloria canitiem.

IX

Dicebam tibi uenturos, irrisor, amores,
   nec tibi perpetuo libera uerba fore:

26 hylaeis *V2*: ellaeis *DV1Vo.*: hi(l)leis *et similia NAFP*
VIIIb *sequentia non separant codices, separauit Lipsius*

ecce iaces supplexque uenis ad iura puellae,
  et tibi nunc quaeuis imperat empta modo.
non me Chaoniae uincant in amore columbae   5
  dicere, quos iuuenes quaeque puella domet.
me dolor et lacrimae merito fecere peritum:
  atque utinam posito dicar amore rudis!
quid tibi nunc misero prodest graue dicere carmen
  aut Amphioniae moenia flere lyrae?   10
plus in amore ualet Mimnermi uersus Homero:
  carmina mansuetus lenia quaerit Amor.
i quaeso et tristis istos compone libellos,
  et cane quod quaeuis nosse puella uelit!
quid si non esset facilis tibi copia? nunc tu   15
  insanus medio flumine quaeris aquam.
necdum etiam palles, uero nec tangeris igni:
  haec est uenturi prima fauilla mali.
tum magis Armenias cupies accedere tigris
  et magis infernae uincula nosse rotae,   20
quam pueri totiens arcum sentire medullis
  et nihil iratae posse negare tuae.
nullus Amor cuiquam facilis ita praebuit alas,
  ut non alterna presserit ille manu.
nec te decipiat, quod sit satis illa parata: 25
  acrius illa subit, Pontice, si qua tua est,
quippe ubi non liceat uacuos seducere ocellos,
  nec uigilare alio nomine cedat Amor.
qui non ante patet, donec manus attigit ossa:
  quisquis es, assiduas a fuge blanditias!   30
illis et silices et possint cedere quercus,
  nedum tu possis, spiritus iste leuis.
quare, si pudor est, quam primum errata fatere:
  dicere quo pereas saepe in amore leuat.

30 a fuge *Bolt*: aufuge *O*

X

O iucunda quies, primo cum testis amori
    affueram uestris conscius in lacrimis!
o noctem meminisse mihi iucunda uoluptas,
    o quotiens uotis illa uocanda meis,
cum te complexa morientem, Galle, puella   5
    uidimus et longa ducere uerba mora!
quamuis labentis premeret mihi somnus ocellos
    et mediis caelo Luna ruberet equis,
non tamen a uestro potui secedere lusu:
    tantus in alternis uocibus ardor erat.   10
sed quoniam non es ueritus concredere nobis,
    accipe commissae munera laetitiae:
non solum uestros didici reticere dolores,
    est quiddam in nobis maius, amice, fide.
possum ego diuersos iterum coniungere amantis,   15
    et dominae tardas possum aperire fores;
et possum alterius curas sanare recentis,
    nec leuis in uerbis est medicina meis.
Cynthia me docuit semper quaecumque petenda
    quaeque cauenda forent: non nihil egit amor.   20
tu caue ne tristi cupias pugnare puellae,
    neue superba loqui, neue tacere diu;
neu, si quid petiit, ingrata fronte negaris,
    neu tibi pro uano uerba benigna cadant.
irritata uenit, quando contemnitur illa,   25
    nec meminit iustas ponere laesa minas:
at quo sis humilis magis et subiectus amori,
    hoc magis effectu saepe fruare bono.
is poterit felix una remanere puella,
    qui numquam uacuo pectore liber erit.   30

11 concredere *V*ː: concedere *O*   28 effectu ς: effecto *O*

XI

Ecquid te mediis cessantem, Cynthia, Bais,
    qua iacet Herculeis semita litoribus,
et modo Thesproti mirantem subdita regno
    proxima Misenis aequora nobilibus,
nostri cura subit memores, a, ducere noctes?   5
    ecquis in extremo restat amore locus?
an te nescio quis simulatis ignibus hostis
    sustulit e nostris, Cynthia, carminibus?
atque utinam mage te remis confisa minutis
    paruula Lucrina cumba moretur aqua,   10
aut teneat clausam tenui Teuthrantis in unda
    alternae facilis cedere lympha manu,
quam uacet alterius blandos audire susurros
    molliter in tacito litore compositam!—
ut solet amoto labi custode puella,   15
    perfida communis nec meminisse deos:
non quia perspecta non es mihi cognita fama,
    sed quod in hac omnis parte timetur amor.
ignosces igitur, si quid tibi triste libelli
    attulerint nostri: culpa timoris erit.   20
an mihi nunc maior carae custodia matris?
    aut sine te uitae cura sit ulla meae?
tu mihi sola domus, tu, Cynthia, sola parentes,
    omnia tu nostrae tempora laetitiae.
seu tristis ueniam seu contra laetus amicis,   25
    quicquid ero, dicam 'Cynthia causa fuit.'
tu modo quam primum corruptas desere Baias:
    multis ista dabunt litora discidium,

---

5 ah ducere *Scaliger*: adducere *O*   11 Teuthrantis *Scaliger*: teutantis *et similia* codd.   15 amoto *PDVVo.*: amota *NAF*   21 nunc *Beck*: non *O*

litora quae fuerunt castis inimica puellis:
   a pereant Baiae, crimen amoris, aquae!   30

XII

Quid mihi desidiae non cessas fingere crimen,
   quod faciat nobis conscia Roma moram?
tam multa illa meo diuisa est milia lecto,
   quantum Hypanis Veneto dissidet Eridano;
nec mihi consuetos amplexu nutrit amores   5
   Cynthia, nec nostra dulcis in aure sonat.
olim gratus eram: non illo tempore cuiquam
   contigit ut simili posset amare fide.
inuidiae fuimus: num me deus obruit? an quae
   lecta Prometheis diuidit herba iugis?   10
non sum ego qui fueram: mutat uia longa puellas.
   quantus in exiguo tempore fugit amor!
nunc primum longas solus cognoscere noctes
   cogor et ipse meis auribus esse grauis.
felix, qui potuit praesenti flere puellae;   15
   non nihil aspersis gaudet Amor lacrimis:
aut si despectus potuit mutare calores,
   sunt quoque translato gaudia seruitio.
mi neque amare aliam neque ab hac desistere fas est:
   Cynthia prima fuit, Cynthia finis erit.   20

XIII

Tu, quod saepe soles, nostro laetabere casu,
   Galle, quod abrepto solus amore uacem.
at non ipse tuas imitabor, perfide, uoces:
   fallere te numquam, Galle, puella uelit.

29 fuerunt *Scaliger*: fuerant *O*
XII *sequentia non separant codices plerique*   2 facias *Bailey* (conscia Roma
pro uoc. accipiens)   9 num *F₄V*: non *codd. plerique*

dum tibi deceptis augetur fama puellis,　　　　　　5
　certus et in nullo quaeris amore moram,
perditus in quadam tardis pallescere curis
　incipis, et primo lapsus abire gradu.
haec erit illarum contempti poena doloris:
　multarum miseras exiget una uices.　　　　　　10
haec tibi uulgaris istos compescet amores,
　nec noua quaerendo semper amicus eris.
haec ego non rumore malo, non augure doctus;
　uidi ego: me quaeso teste negare potes?
uidi ego te toto uinctum languescere collo　　　　15
　et flere iniectis, Galle, diu manibus,
et cupere optatis animam deponere uerbis,
　et quae deinde meus celat, amice, pudor.
non ego complexus potui diducere uestros:
　tantus erat demens inter utrosque furor.　　　　20
non sic Haemonio Salmonida mixtus Enipeo
　Taenarius facili pressit amore deus,
nec sic caelestem flagrans amor Herculis Heben
　sensit in Oetaeis gaudia prima iugis.
una dies omnis potuit praecurrere amantis:　　　25
　nam tibi non tepidas subdidit illa faces,
nec tibi praeteritos passa est succedere fastus,
　nec sinet abduci: te tuus ardor aget.
nec mirum, cum sit Ioue digna et proxima Ledae
　et Ledae partu gratior, una tribus;　　　　　　30
illa sit Inachiis et blandior heroinis,
　illa suis uerbis cogat amare Iouem.
tu uero quoniam semel es periturus amore,
　utere: non alio limine dignus eras.
qui tibi sit felix, quoniam nouus incidit, error;　　35
　et, quodcumque uoles, una sit ista tibi.

---

8 abire *V2*: adire O　　17 uerbis *O*: labris *codd. Passeratii*　　24 in *O*:
ab *Scaliger*　　35 qui *Palmer:* quae *O*

XIV

Tu licet abiectus Tiberina molliter unda
  Lesbia Mentoreo uina bibas opere,
et modo tam celeres mireris currere lintres
  et modo tam tardas funibus ire ratis;
et nemus omne satas intendat uertice siluas,   5
  urgetur quantis Caucasus arboribus;
non tamen ista meo ualeant contendere amori:
  nescit amor magnis cedere diuitiis.
nam siue optatam mecum trahit illa quietem,
  seu facili totum ducit amore diem,   10
tum mihi Pactoli ueniunt sub tecta liquores,
  et legitur Rubris gemma sub aequoribus;
tum mihi cessuros spondent mea gaudia reges:
  quae maneant, dum me fata perire uolent!
nam quis diuitiis aduerso gaudet Amore?   15
  nulla mihi tristi praemia sint Venere!
illa potest magnas heroum infringere uires,
  illa etiam duris mentibus esse dolor:
illa neque Arabium metuit transcendere limen
  nec timet ostrino, Tulle, subire toro,   20
et miserum toto iuuenem uersare cubili:
  quid releuant uariis serica textilibus?
quae mihi dum placata aderit, non ulla uerebor
  regna uel Alcinoi munera despicere.

XV

Saepe ego multa tuae leuitatis dura timebam,
  hac tamen excepta, Cynthia, perfidia.
aspice me quanto rapiat fortuna periclo!
  tu tamen in nostro lenta timore uenis;

5 ut tendat *Rothstein*

et potes hesternos manibus componere crinis   5
   et longa faciem quaerere desidia,
nec minus Eois pectus uariare lapillis,
   ut formosa nouo quae parat ire uiro.
at non sic Ithaci digressu mota Calypso
   desertis olim fleuerat aequoribus: 10
multos illa dies incomptis maesta capillis
   sederat, iniusto multa locuta salo,
et quamuis numquam post haec uisura, dolebat
   illa tamen, longae conscia laetitiae.   14
néc sic Aesoniden rapientibus anxia uentis   17
   Hypsipyle uacuo constitit in thalamo: 18
Hypsipyle nullos post illos sensit amores,   19
   ut semel Haemonio tabuit hospitio.   20
coniugis Euadne miseros elata per ignis   21
   occidit, Argiuae fama pudicitiae.
Alphesiboea suos ulta est pro coniuge fratres,   15
   sanguinis et cari uincula rupit amor.   16
quarum nulla tuos potuit conuertere mores,
   tu quoque uti fieres nobilis historia.
desine iam reuocare tuis periuria uerbis,   25
   Cynthia, et oblitos parce mouere deos;
audax a nimium, nostro dolitura periclo,
   si quid forte tibi durius inciderit!
nulla prius uasto labentur flumina ponto,
   annus et inuersas duxerit ante uices,   30
quam tua sub nostro mutetur pectore cura:
   sis quodcumque uoles, non aliena tamen.
tam tibi ne uiles isti uideantur ocelli,
   per quos saepe mihi credita perfidia est!

---

7 eois *PDVVo.*: et chois *N*: *alii codd. alia*   15-16 *post* 22 *Lachmann*: *post* 20 *Markland*   21 elata *O*: delata ç   29 nulla *codd. Passeratii*: multa *O*   33 tam tibi *Palmer*: quam tibi *O*

hos tu iurabas, si quid mentita fuisses,   35
    ut tibi suppositis exciderent manibus:
et contra magnum potes hos attollere Solem,
    nec tremis admissae conscia nequitiae?
quis te cogebat multos pallere colores
    et fletum inuitis ducere luminibus?   40
quis ego nunc pereo, similis moniturus amantis
    'O nullis tutum credere blanditiis!'

XVI

'Quae fueram magnis olim patefacta triumphis,
    ianua Tarpeiae nota pudicitiae;
cuius inaurati celebrarunt limina currus,
    captorum lacrimis umida supplicibus;
nunc ego, nocturnis potorum saucia rixis,   5
    pulsata indignis saepe queror manibus,
et mihi non desunt turpes pendere corollae
    semper et exclusi signa iacere faces.
nec possum infamis dominae defendere noctes,
    nobilis obscenis tradita carminibus;   10
nec tamen illa suae reuocatur parcere famae,
    turpior et saecli uiuere luxuria.
has inter grauibus cogor deflere querelis,
    supplicis a longis tristior excubiis.
ille meos numquam patitur requiescere postis,   15
    arguta referens carmina blanditia:
"Ianua uel domina penitus crudelior ipsa,
    quid mihi tam duris clausa taces foribus?
cur numquam reserata meos admittis amores,
    nescia furtiuas reddere mota preces?   20
nullane finis erit nostro concessa dolori,
    turpis et in tepido limine somnus erit?

XVI 8 exclusi *Lipsius*: exclusis *O*

me mediae noctes, me sidera plena iacentem,
  frigidaque Eoo me dolet aura gelu:
tu sola humanos numquam miserata dolores   25
  respondes tacitis mutua cardinibus.
o utinam traiecta caua mea uocula rima
  percussas dominae uertat in auriculas!
sit licet et saxo patientior illa Sicano,
  sit licet et ferro durior et chalybe,   30
non tamen illa suos poterit compescere ocellos,
  surget et inuitis spiritus in lacrimis.
nunc iacet alterius felici nixa lacerto,
  at mea nocturno uerba cadunt Zephyro.
sed tu sola mei tu maxima causa doloris,   35
  uicta meis numquam, ianua, muneribus.
te non ulla meae laesit petulantia linguae,
  quae solet †ingrato dicere pota loco†,
ut me tam longa raucum patiare querela
  sollicitas triuio peruigilare moras.   40
at tibi saepe nouo deduxi carmina uersu,
  osculaque impressis nixa dedi gradibus.
ante tuos quotiens uerti me, perfida, postis,
  debitaque occultis uota tuli manibus!"
haec ille et si quae miseri nouistis amantes,   45
  et matutinis obstrepit alitibus.
sic ego nunc dominae uitiis et semper amantis
  fletibus aeterna differor inuidia.'

XVII

Et merito, quoniam potui fugisse puellam,
  nunc ego desertas alloquor alcyonas.

---

23 plena *O*: prona ς   noctis *Housman*   38 ingrato *Fruter*: irato *O*
pota *Heinsius*: tota *O*   48 differor *V2*: deferor *O*

nec mihi Cassiope saluo uisura carinam,
    omniaque ingrato litore uota cadunt.
quin etiam absenti prosunt tibi, Cynthia, uenti: 5
    aspice, quam saeuas increpat aura minas.
nullane placatae ueniet fortuna procellae?
    haecine parua meum funus harena teget?
tu tamen in melius saeuas conuerte querelas:
    sat tibi sit poenae nox et iniqua uada.   10
an poteris siccis mea fata reponere ocellis,
    ossaque nulla tuo nostra tenere sinu?
a pereat, quicumque ratis et uela parauit
    primus et inuito gurgite fecit iter!
nonne fuit leuius dominae peruincere mores   15
    (quamuis dura, tamen rara puella fuit),
quam sic ignotis circumdata litora siluis
    cernere et optatos quaerere Tyndaridas?
illic si qua meum sepelissent fata dolorem,
    ultimus et posito staret amore lapis,   20
illa meo caros donasset funere crinis,
    molliter et tenera poneret ossa rosa;
illa meum extremo clamasset puluere nomen,
    ut mihi non ullo pondere terra foret.
at uos, aequoreae formosa Doride natae,   25
    candida felici soluite uela choro:
si quando uestras labens Amor attigit undas,
    mansuetis socio parcite litoribus.

XVIII

Haec certe deserta loca et taciturna querenti,
    et uacuum Zephyri possidet aura nemus.
hic licet occultos proferre impune dolores,
    si modo sola queant saxa tenere fidem.

XVII 3 saluo *Richmond*: solito O   11 reponere O: reposcere *Baehrens*

36

unde tuos primum repetam, mea Cynthia, fastus?   5
   quod mihi das flendi, Cynthia, principium?
qui modo felices inter numerabar amantis,
   nunc in amore tuo cogor habere notam.
quid tantum merui? quae te mihi crimina mutant?
   an noua tristitiae causa puella tuae?   10
sic mihi te referas, leuis, ut non altera nostro
   limine formosos intulit ulla pedes.
quamuis multa tibi dolor hic meus aspera debet,
   non ita saeua tamen uenerit ira mea,
ut tibi sim merito semper furor, et tua flendo   15
   lumina deiectis turpia sint lacrimis.
an quia parua damus mutato signa colore,
   et non ulla meo clamat in ore fides?
uos eritis testes, si quos habet arbor amores,
   fagus et Arcadio pinus amica deo.   20
a quotiens teneras resonant mea uerba sub umbras,
   scribitur et uestris Cynthia corticibus!
an tua quod peperit nobis iniuria curas,
   quae solum tacitis cognita sunt foribus?
omnia consueui timidus perferre superbae   25
   iussa neque arguto facta dolore queri.
pro quo diuini fontes et frigida rupes
   et datur inculto tramite dura quies;
et quodcumque meae possunt narrare querelae,
   cogor ad argutas dicere solus auis.   30
sed qualiscumque es resonent mihi 'Cynthia' siluae,
   nec deserta tuo nomine saxa uacent.

XIX

Non ego nunc tristis uereor, mea Cynthia, Manis,
   nec moror extremo debita fata rogo;

9 crimina ς: carmina O   27 diuini *codd.*: *coniec. alii alia*

sed ne forte tuo careat mihi funus amore,
  hic timor est ipsis durior exsequiis.
non adeo leuiter nostris puer haesit ocellis,   5
  ut meus oblito puluis amore uacet.
illic Phylacides iucundae coniugis heros
  non potuit caecis immemor esse locis,
sed cupidus falsis attingere gaudia palmis
  Thessalus antiquam uenerat umbra domum.   10
illic quidquid ero, semper tua dicar imago:
  traicit et fati litora magnus amor.
illic formosae ueniant chorus heroinae,
  quas dedit Argiuis Dardana praeda uiris—
quarum nulla tua fuerit mihi, Cynthia, forma   15
  gratior; et (Tellus hoc ita iusta sinat)
quamuis te longae remorentur fata senectae,
  cara tamen lacrimis ossa futura meis.
quae tu uiua mea possis sentire fauilla!
  tum mihi non ullo mors sit amara loco.   20
quam uereor, ne te contempto, Cynthia, busto
  abstrahat, heu, nostro puluere iniquus amor,
cogat et inuitam lacrimas siccare cadentis!
  flectitur assiduis certa puella minis.
quare, dum licet, inter nos laetemur amantes: 25
  non satis est ullo tempore longus amor.

XX

Hoc pro continuo te, Galle, monemus amore,
  (id tibi ne uacuo defluat ex animo)
saepe imprudenti fortuna occurrit amanti:
  crudelis Minyis dixerit Ascanius.
est tibi non infra speciem, non nomine dispar,   5
  Theiodamanteo proximus ardor Hylae:

17 te longae *codd. plerique*: longe te *NA*   22 heu *Hertzberg*: e *O*
XX 5 specie *Heinsius*

huic tu, siue leges umbrosae flumina siluae,
  siue Aniena tuos tinxerit unda pedes,
siue Gigantea spatiabere litoris ora,
  siue ubicumque uago fluminis hospitio,   10
Nympharum semper cupidas defende rapinas
  (non minor Ausoniis est amor Adryasin);
ne tibi sint duri montes et frigida saxa,
  Galle, neque expertos semper adire lacus:
quae miser ignotis error perpessus in oris   15
  Herculis indomito fleuerat Ascanio.
namque ferunt olim Pagasae naualibus Argon
  egressam longe Phasidcs isse uiam,
et iam praeteritis labentem Athamantidos undis
  Mysorum scopulis applicuisse ratem.   20
hic manus heroum, placidis ut constitit oris,
  mollia composita litora fronde tegit.
at comes inuicti iuuenis processerat ultra
  raram sepositi quaerere fontis aquam.
hunc duo sectati fratres, Aquilonia proles,   25
  hunc super et Zetes, hunc super et Calais,
oscula suspensis instabant carpere palmis,
  oscula et alterna ferre supina fuga.
ille sub extrema pendens secluditur ala
  et uolucres ramo summouet insidias.   30
iam Pandioniae cessit genus Orithyiae:
  a dolor! ibat Hylas, ibat Hamadryasin.
hic erat Arganthi Pege sub uertice montis
  grata domus Nymphis umida Thyniasin,
quam supra nullae pendebant debita curae   35
  roscida desertis poma sub arboribus,

---

7 huic *Auratus*: hunc *siue* nunc *codd.*   12 Adryasin *Struve*: adriacis O
13 sint duri O: sit duros *codd. Heinsii*   31 cessit ς: cesset O
32 Hamadryasin *edd.*: (h)amadriss hinc O   33 Pege *Turnebus*: phege O

et circum irriguo surgebant lilia prato
  candida purpureis mixta papaueribus.
quae modo decerpens tenero pueriliter ungui
  proposito florem praetulit officio,   40
et modo formosis incumbens nescius undis
  errorem blandis tardat imaginibus.
tandem haurire parat demissis flumina palmis
  innixus dextro plena trahens umero.
cuius ut accensae Dryades candore puellae   45
  miratae solitos destituere choros,
prolapsum leuiter facili traxere liquore:
  tum sonitum rapto corpore fecit Hylas.
cui procul Alcides iterat responsa, sed illi
  nomen ab extremis fontibus aura refert.   50
his, o Galle, tuos monitus seruabis amores,
  formosum Nymphis credere uisus Hylan.

XXI

'Tu, qui consortem properas euadere casum,
  miles ab Etruscis saucius aggeribus,
quid nostro gemitu turgentia lumina torques?
  pars ego sum uestrae proxima militiae.
sic te seruato possint gaudere parentes: 5
  me soror Acca tuis sentiat e lacrimis,
Gallum, per medios ereptum Caesaris ensis
  effugere ignotas non potuisse manus;
et quaecumque super dispersa inuenerit ossa
  montibus Etruscis, haec sciat esse mea.'   10

50 fontibus O: montibus *Heinsius*
XXI 5 sic te seruato possint *Passerat*: sic te seruato ut possint O   6 me
Sluiter: ne O   Acca *Scaliger*: acta O

XXII

Qualis et unde genus, qui sint mihi, Tulle, Penates,
   quaeris pro nostra semper amicitia.
si Perusina tibi patriae sunt nota sepulcra,
   Italiae duris funera temporibus,
cum Romana suos egit discordia ciuis—   5
   sed mihi praecipue, puluis Etrusca, dolor:
tu proiecta mei perpessa es membra propinqui,
   tu nullo miseri contegis ossa solo—
proxima supposito contingens Vmbria campo
   me genuit terris fertilis uberibus.   10

XXII *sequentia non separat N*   6 sed (sct) *Palmer*: sit O

NOTES

I

A poem of tormented feeling, of the kind of which Cat. LXXXV
is the most famous example. The poet is prisoner of a passion
from which, at least with half of himself, he longs to be free.

Of the motives used in developing the theme a number
resemble motives that are used also by Tibullus and Horace,
though not in identical applications. Compare for instance lines
1–4 with Tib. II, iv, 1–4, line 7 with Tib. II, v, 109, lines 9 ff.
with Tib. I, iv, 47–50, lines 19 and 24 with Tib. I, ii, 45–6,
line 25 with Hor. *Epod.* xi, 25–6, lines 27–8 with Tib. I, v, 5–6
(where Tibullus desires as punishment for his failing the same
painful treatment that Propertius desires as a means of libera-
tion), line 33 with Tib. II, iv, 11.

Further, lines 1–4 recall in details the opening lines of *A.P.*
XII, ci, an epigram of Meleager:

> Τόν με πόθοις ἄτρωτον ὑπὸ στέρνοισι Μυΐσκος
> ὄμμασι τοξεύσας τοῦτ' ἐβόησεν ἔπος·
> Τὸν θρασὺν εἶλον ἐγώ· τὸ δ' ἐπ' ὀφρύσι κεῖνο φρύαγμα
> σκηπτροφόρου σοφίας ἠνίδε ποσσὶ πατῶ.

New phases in the development of the thought begin with
lines 9, 19 and 29 (or 31).

1–2. prima...nullis ante cupidinibus: at III, xv, 1 ff.
Propertius says that his first experience of love was with a certain
Lycinna. But it was not what he now understands by love.

2. contactum: this word combines the associations of two
meanings that it bears in other contexts: 'hit' by a missile, and
'infected' with a disease.

3. tum mihi constantis deiecit lumina fastus: this can
be rendered either (*a*) 'quelled my look of stubborn pride'
(*fastus* being genitive of quality or definition); or (*b*) 'forced
my stubborn pride to lower its eyes' (*fastus* being possessive
genitive, and the notion of 'pride' being half-personified).

5–6. castas odisse puellas, etc.: 'to have no use for women
who are not free with their favours, and to lead a reckless life'.

This could refer either to the poet's way of living in the company of Cynthia and her friends (cf. I, iv, 25–7, II, vi, 1 ff., II, xxxii, 29 ff., etc.), or to his seeking lower company as a result of unkindness on her part (cf. II, xxiii, II, xxiv, 9, etc.). The present poem purports to be written at a time when P.'s relations with Cynthia were unhappy. *castus, -a* is a less specific word than 'chaste', and could apply, for instance, to a courtesan who kept for a time to one man. *odi* here is less than 'hate'.

9 ff. Milanion: the successful wooer of Atalanta daughter of Iasus (or Iasius). Atalanta, who had been exposed in infancy on Mount Parthenius in Arcadia and suckled by a she-bear, was extremely fleet of foot (cf. *uelocem* in line 15) and lived as a huntress in the Arcadian hills, where on a certain occasion two centaurs named Hylaeus and Rhoeteus tried to molest her. There was also a famous story, not mentioned by Propertius here, that Atalanta challenged all her suitors to race against her, and that Milanion succeeded by dropping three golden apples, which she could not resist stopping to pick up. [Another form of the legend places Atalanta in Boeotia, not Arcadia, and makes her successful suitor Hippomenes, not Milanion.]

Tulle: see on I, vi, 2 below.

11–13. nam modo...ibat et...ille etiam...: with this series compare I, iii, 41–3 *nam modo...rursus et...interdum.* The present passage is said to be the only one in classical Latin poetry in which *modo* = 'sometimes' in the first member of a series has not corresponding to it in the second member a word such as *modo, saepe, tum, rursus,* etc.

11. antris here = 'rocky glens', as sometimes elsewhere in poetry (see Housman on Manilius v, 311). The word more regularly means a grotto, or the space sheltered by an overhanging rock.

12. ibat...uidere: this infinitive of purpose or result after a verb of motion is not found in classical prose, but there are several instances in the Augustan poets. Cf. in this book vi, 33, xi, 5, xx, 24.

uidere can here be rendered 'to brave'. The Latin can keep the simple verb of experience and let the fact that the experience is a formidable one be sufficiently conveyed by the context: cf. Virg. *Aen.* VI, 134 *bis nigra uidere Tartara*; III, 431 *informem uasto uidisse sub antro Scyllam.* In English 'see' is not enough.

13. rami here stands for 'club'. The same word is used of

Hercules' club at IV, ix, 15. [But Ovid, *A.A.* II, 191, speaks of *Hylaei...arcum.*]

14. Arcadiis rupibus: this may be ablative of place, or dative, or both: cf. I, xx, 16 (and, for a double construction, note on I, xix, 6).

15. domuisse: the perfect infinitive is used here, as often in the elegiac poets, simply as a metrically convenient synonym for the present infinitive. It does not indicate a time past in relation to *potuit*.

16. tantum...ualent: this is the general rule illustrated by the experience of Milanion which he has just cited. But his own case, he goes on to say, is an exception to the general rule.

preces: he has not actually said that Milanion made use of these, but he can easily enough expect us to assume it. He probably has in mind the standard figure of the devoted and imploring lover, and having dwelt so much, in his illustration, on the first of these attributes he has forgotten that he did not illustrate the second.

19. deductae...fallacia lunae: 'the trick of drawing down the moon'. *fallacia* is often used in comedy for the tricks and contrivances of the ingenious slave; in Virg. *Georg.* IV, 443 it is used of the magic whereby Proteus turns himself into fire, water, animal forms, etc. The value of the genitive *deductae... lunae* is as in I, xvii, 7 *placatae...fortuna procellae*, or Virg. *Aen.* I, 27 *spretaeque iniuria formae*. The word *fallacia* suggests of course deceit or illusion, and Propertius may have intended this, for cf. the scepticism of the witches' powers implied in lines 23–4. But the phrase is really ambiguous; a keen analyst may press the distinction between the illusions created by a conjuror and the real miracles performed by a magician, but under which heading shall we classify the *fallaciae* of Proteus in *Georg.* IV, 443?

20. sacra piare: the usual meaning of *piare* is to appease (divine displeasure) or expiate (a religious offence) by the performance of *sacra*. In its context here and with *sacra* for object it evidently = 'perform' with a special overtone, very likely the idea of an elaborate and exact ritual.

[The ironical use of a word with holy associations in an unholy context is not un-Propertian; for cf. III, xix, 17–18 *matris iram natorum caede piauit amor.*]

23. crediderim uobis...posse...: 'believe your claim that you can...'.

24. Cytinaeis: Cytina was a town in Thessaly, mentioned by Lycophron, *Alexandra* 1389, where the quantity of the second syllable is attested by the metre. Hence *Cytinaeis* is a plausible though not certain correction of the corrupt text given at this point by our MSS. Its meaning will be 'Thessalian', the town standing for the country as often in Augustan poets, and the witches of Thessaly being a byword: cf. III, xxiv, 10 *Thessala saga*, in a passage which seems to echo this one.

[Some read here *Cytaeines*, as the witch Medea is called *Cytaeis* —woman of Cytaea, in Colchis—by Propertius at II, iv, 17. The form *Cytaeine* would be an alternative to *Cytaeis* as *Nereine* is to *Nereis*, and *Cytaeines* would be its (Greek) genitive. For the suitability of this form here cf. Ov. *Met.* VIII, 528 *matres Calydonides Eueninae* (living near the river Euenus); and for the genitive construction cf. Tib. I, ii, 51 *sola tenere malas Medeae dicitur herbas*.]

31. facili deus annuit aure: the jump in thought between *aure* and *annuit* is characteristic of Propertius.

33. in me nostra Venus noctes exercet amaras: here *nostra Venus* could mean either (*a*) 'Venus whom I (*or* we lovers) serve'; or (*b*) 'the thought of her whom I love', *Venus* being taken as in Virg. *Ecl.* III, 68 *parta meae Veneri sunt munera*. The former meaning—'my (*or* our) mistress Venus'— is here more probable, in view of I, xiv, 16 ff.

noctes exercet amaras could mean either (*a*) 'troubles my nights and makes them wretched', *amaras* being taken proleptically and *exercet* as in Virg. *Georg.* IV, 453 *non te nullius exercent numinis irae*; or (*b*) 'works (i.e. brings about) nights of torment', *exercet* being taken as in Virg. *Aen.* IV, 99 *quin potius pacem aeternam pactosque hymenaeos exercemus?*

[The fact that *nostra* stands next to *me* does not, in itself, create a probability that a contrast is intended and so that *nostra* here means 'our'; for cf. II, xxxii, 23 *nuper enim de te nostras me laedit ad aures rumor*.]

34. et nullo uacuus tempore defit amor: 'and love never rests or ceases'.

35. hoc...malum: 'this plague'.

II

In form this is a lecture to Cynthia. Its principal motive resembles one that appears (in a different application) in Tib. I, viii, 9–16:

> quid tibi nunc molles prodest coluisse capillos
> saepeque mutatas disposuisse comas;
> quid fuco splendente genas ornare, quid ungues
> artificis docta subsecuisse manu?
> frustra iam uestes, frustra mutantur amictus
> ansaque compressos colligit arta pedes.

The same motive is introduced again, in Elegy xv, another lecture to Cynthia, in a different setting.

1. ornato...capillo: *ornato* here means '(elaborately) arranged'; cf. Ov. *Am.* I, xiv, 5 (*capilli*) *tenues et quos ornare timeres.*

2. Coa ueste: Coan silks were noted for their fineness and transparency. (The caterpillar that produced the raw material for them was not the same as the silkworm that we know.)

sinus: poets use *sinus* in an extended sense, both in singular and plural, to mean simply a woman's dress or gown; cf. Ov. *Fast.* v, 28; Tib. I, ix, 70; Ov. *Her.* XIII, 36. (It may be that the idea of a flowing or billowing dress is included.)

Coa...ueste...sinus: for this ablative of the material of which the *sinus* consist cf. Virg. *Ecl.* III, 39 *diffusos hedera...pallente corymbos.*

3. Orontea: 'Syrian', after the river Orontes in Syria.

4. teque...uendere: 'set off your charms', as a vendor sets off his wares to make them as attractive as possible; for a similar idiomatic use of *uendere* cf. Hor. *Epist.* II, i, 4–5 *si uersus ...concinnior unus et alter...totum...uendit...poema*; and for a somewhat similar one cf. Juvenal VII, 135 *purpura uendit* (= 'advertises') *causidicum.*

muneribus: this can hardly here mean 'gifts'. It must be used in an extended sense, and mean 'finery' or the like.

7. non ulla tuae est medicina figurae: i.e. no doctoring can make your appearance more beautiful than it already is. The word *medicina* seems normally to be used of what remedies an undesirable condition and not of what produces or enhances a desirable one; but the Greek φάρμακον can be used in both senses and it may well be that here *medicina* = φάρμακον and *figura* = μορφή.

[The most authoritative manuscripts here read *non ulla tua est....* If we keep that, the meaning will be 'your doctoring of your looks is trouble wasted'. The resolution of a negative word like *nullus* into a positive word and a preceding negative particle is a favourite mannerism of Propertius; cf. II, xxviii, 52 *Europe nec proba Pasiphae*; II, xii, 8 *nostraque non ullis permanet aura locis*; I, vi, 23 *non umquam*, etc. For *nullus* = 'worthless' or the like cf. Cic. *Acad.* II, xcvi *aut quidquid igitur eodem modo concluditur probabitis aut ars ista* (logic) *nulla est.*]

8. nudus amor: the adjective gives a reason for Love's attitude to dressing-up. Cupid is depicted nude.

11. solis...in antris: 'in lonely glens'; i.e. in wild conditions. For the meaning of *antris* cf. on I, i, 11.

13. litora natiuis persuadent picta lapillis: the meaning required by the context is 'beaches made gay by nature's own mosaics are charming to the eye'. But it is much disputed whether the sense required can be extracted from *persuadent*.

lapillis: mosaics, as in Hor. *Ep.*I, x, 19 *Libycis . . . lapillis.* This is here a metaphor for the sea-shells, which are said in Lucr. II, 375 *pingere telluris gremium.*

15–16. Phoebe and **Hilaira** were daughters of Leucippus, a legendary king of Messenia. Castor and Pollux fought over them with the sons of Aphareus, Lynceus and Idas.

15. non sic: i.e. *non cultu.*

17–18. Euenus had a daughter named Marpessa, who was carried off by Idas (see on 15–16). Pursuing them Euenus fell into a river in Aetolia, which was thenceforth named after him. When later Apollo tried to take Marpessa from Idas, Jupiter (= Zeus) let her choose between them, and she chose the man rather than the god because he would grow old with her.

17. discordia: i.e. an *object of* strife.

19–20. Oenomaus King of Elis obliged all applicants for the hand of his daughter Hippodamia to compete with him in a chariot-race, with the penalty of death if they were defeated. Pelops coming from Phrygia induced the king's groom to remove (according to one account) a linchpin from his master's chariot, with the result that Oenomaus was killed and Pelops acquired both his daughter and his kingdom.

21. obnoxia: 'indebted to'; cf. Virg. *Georg.* I, 396 *fratris radiis obnoxia... Luna.*

22. qualis...color...: one can supply in thought with *facies* in the preceding line *tali colore* (as an epithet) or *color* (in apposition).

Apelleis: by the famous Coan painter Apelles, of the fourth century B.C.

25–6. non ego nunc...sat est: the thought seems to be: 'after all, I am the one you really mind about and want to please; you neither need nor ought to get yourself up to please other men'. The first sentence is a meiosis and really means 'I know very well that I am much more important to you than your other admirers'.

25. istis: Cynthia's other admirers; cf. for the existence of them II, vi, 1 ff., and for the use of *isti* I, viii, 3 and II, ix, 1.

27–8. libens: this goes with *Phoebus* as well as with *Calliopea*.

28. Calliopea: later the muse of epic, but in Propertius' day the Muses were not yet rigidly specialized. Here one could fairly translate 'the Muse'.

30. omnia...probat: there are alternative ways of taking this: (*a*) *omnia* is in apposition to the content of line 29, or of lines 27–9; or (*b*) *omnia quaeque* stands for *omniaque quae...*, and adds a new group of items.

31. nostrae uitae: 'to me always', cf. I, vi, 21 *nam tua non aetas umquam cessauit amori*; I, xiii, 23 *amor Herculis...sensit gaudia*, etc.

III

A scene, the central feature of which recalls the opening of *A.P.* v, cxxiii, an epigram of Philodemus:

> νυκτερινή, δίκερως, φιλοπάννυχε, φαῖνε, Σελήνη·
> φαῖνε, δι' εὐτρήτων βαλλομένη θυρίδων.
> αὔγαζε χρυσέην Καλλίστιον....

The complaint of Cynthia in lines 35–46 is the converse of the lover's complaint that will be found in Elegy XVI, lines 17–44.

2. Cnosia: Ariadne, of Cnossos in Crete, who enabled

48

Theseus to escape from the labyrinth and was later left by him marooned on Naxos.

3. accubuit: this verb (with or without a dative), is used normally, by other authors, of those who recline at table, not of those who lie at rest. Propertius favours the unusual in his choice of compound verbs; cf. I, iv, 27 *adoro*, and note on I, vii, 15. But cf. also Tib. I, ix, 75 *huic tamen accubuit noster puer*.

3–4. Andromede, daughter of Cepheus king of Ethiopia, was chained to a rock and exposed to be eaten by a sea-monster but rescued by Perseus in the nick of time.

5. Edonis: 'Thracian woman' (nom. sing. fem.), the Edones (or Edoni) being a people of Thrace. The poet has in mind a Thracian bacchante exhausted after an ecstasy.

6. Apidano: the Apidanus was a river in Thessaly, tributary of the Peneus.

in herboso concidit Apidano: here *in* must (unusually) mean 'beside (the river)'; cf. Virg. *Ecl.* VII, 65–6 *fraxinus in siluis pulcherrima, pinus in hortis, populus in fluuiis*....

[To an Englishman a river-name suggests flowing water; to an Italian it would suggest not only that but also a river-*bed*, dry perhaps partly, at times, and possibly with grass and trees growing in it.]

8. non certis nixa caput manibus: 'her head pillowed on her hands, which lay relaxed (*or* outsprawled)'. For *nixa* in a similar sense cf. I, xvi, 33 *alterius felici nixa lacerto*. For the sense of *non certis* required here by the context cf. Ov. *Am.* I, xi, 1 *colligere incertos et in ordine ponere crines*.

10. quaterent: cf. Ov. *Am.* I, ii, 11 *uidi ego iactatas mota face crescere flammas, et uidi nullo concutiente mori*. The torch needs waving to keep it alight, because at this late hour it is nearly burned out.

11. nondum etiam: a phrase of which Propertius is fond: cf. I, ix, 17, etc. It means no more than simple *nondum*.

16. osculaque admota sumere et arma manu: 'to steal a kiss and venture a caress'. *sumere oscula* and *sumere arma* are both regular expressions, but as *sumere* has not the same meaning in both, and as the latter is here used metaphorically, the combination of them produces the effect of a zeugma. For *arma* used metaphorically with reference to a phase of love-making cf. III, xx, 19–20 *ante...dulcia quam nobis concitet arma Venus*.

[The phrase *sumere arma* means of course literally 'to take up arms'. It looks here as though it were a piece of jargon current among Propertius' friends, and used by them in some such sense as 'go to work' or, more specifically, 'start making love'. For the probable point of *admota...manu* cf. Plaut. *Bacch.* 480.]

17. ausus eram: Propertius often makes the pluperfect do duty for preterite or imperfect.

18. expertae: the perfect participle of the deponent *experior* is here used passively; cf. I, xx, 14.

20. Argus ut ignotis cornibus Inachidos: 'as Argus gazed at the strange spectacle of Io horned'. *ignotus* is often used by the poets of what is new to one's experience, and may suggest a reaction of wonder (or alarm, etc.); cf. Ov. *Met.* VIII, 209 (Daedalus) *ignotas umeris accommodat alas*; Virg. *Aen.* III, 591 *ignoti noua forma uiri*.

Argus: the hundred-eyed sentinel set by Juno (= Hera) to keep watch on Io (daughter of Inachus) after Jupiter (= Zeus) had transformed her into a cow.

24. cauis...manibus: the lover brings the gifts piled (cf. line 25 *largibar*) in his hollowed hands. Line 8 shows that *manibus* cannot be dative and refer to Cynthia; cf. also line 26.

25. largibar: alternative form, metrically useful; cf. III, xiii, 35. Parallels are plentiful in comedy, rare in the Augustans.

26. de prono sinu: probably *sinus* here is not used as in I, ii, 2, nor yet as in the passages quoted under I, iv, 14, but means 'bosom', or rather, by an easy extension, 'lap'. *pronus* means here, as often, 'downward sloping'. Cynthia's lap is aslant because she is sleeping on her side. (Alternatively the *sinus* here may be a fold in Cynthia's dress, which looks like a convenient receptacle but gives way under the weight of the fruit and lets it roll out.)

27–8. et quotiens...auspicio: 'and when from time to time you heaved a sigh, I in my timidity took it for an omen, and caught my breath, afraid lest. . . ' [*duxti* is a correction for *duxit* of the best MSS.].

31. diuersas praecurrens luna fenestras: *praecurrere* regularly means 'precede'. Here it is used as if it were a compound of *praeter* (instead of *prae*), to mean 'go by'; cf. *praeuehor* in I, viii, 19 *praeuecta* (fem. sing.) *Ceraunia*, and Tac. *Ann.* II, 6 *Rhenus...qua Germaniam praeuehitur*.

diuersas fenestras: three interpretations are conceivable, but none is demonstrably right. (*a*) 'the open window', referring to the parted shutters. That *fenestra*, like 'window', can denote what fills the aperture as well as the aperture itself is shown by Ov. *Ex Pont.* III, iii, 10 *parvo mota fenestra sono*. But the use of *diuersas* required by this interpretation is not truly paralleled elsewhere; the nearest analogy is in phrases such as Hyginus, *Astr.* II, 6 *palmas diuersas tendere ad caelum*; Prop. I, x, 15 *diuersos* (parted) *iterum coniungere amantes*. (*b*) 'making its round of the windows', the assumption being that there are windows in two or more walls; cf. Stat. *Silu.* II, ii, 75 *diuersis seruit sua terra fenestris*, where windows facing in various directions are said to command each its own view. (*c*) 'the window opposite the bed'. For in Silius Ital. I, 264 *e diuersa ...ripa* means 'on the opposite bank', and in Quint. XI, iii, 133 *diuersa subsellia* means 'the opposite benches', which Q. else-where calls *aduersa subsellia*. However, it must be observed that in both these contexts the idea of 'separation' proper to *diuersus* is appropriate, whereas in the present passage it is not. On the other hand, Propertius seems sometimes deliberately to avoid the normal in his choice of prepositional compounds (e.g. I, vii, 15 *concutere* (*aliquem*) *arcu*, and III, xvi, 16 *percutere faces*; see also on I, iii, 3 *accubuit* and I, iv, 27 *adoro*), so that it is not in-conceivable that he might use *diuersus* as an alternative to *aduersus* (or even to *transuersus*).

32. moraturis: 'laggard'; that is to say 'disposed to linger' or 'that would have lingered if allowed'.

37. meae noctis: 'the night that should have been spent with me'.

38. exactis...sideribus = (by a trope) *exacta nocte*. Cf. Stat. *Theb.* VIII, 219 *uario producunt sidera ludo*.

44. externo longas saepe in amore moras: 'the long hours you spend so often with your other favourites'. For the almost adjectival use of *saepe* cf. I, xxii, 2 *pro nostra semper amicitia* = 'our long friendship'.

45. dum me iucundis lapsam sopor impulit alis: ? 'till sleep [descending] on gentle wing sent me tumbling [into oblivion]'. The expression is so compressed that no interpre-tation can be wholly certain. For a more explicit account of sleep's operation, which may serve as a commentary on this one, see Virg. *Aen.* v, 838–60. Regarding *lapsam*, see also p. 102.

IV

A rebuke (as is also the following Elegy v) to an associate who is supposed to be trying to come between Propertius and Cynthia. Here the intruder is trying to turn Propertius against Cynthia; in v he is setting up as a rival for Cynthia's favour. These two elegies are in outline the same kind of poem as Cat. LXXVII and XCI, in which the poet addresses people who have betrayed his trust in an affair of love. But their content is concerned chiefly with Cynthia and Propertius: Cynthia's beauty and power to charm and to intimidate, and Propertius' total subjection. The detailed motive in lines 13–14 here seems to recall *A.P.* v, cxxxix, 5–6 (Meleager):

> ἢ γάρ μοι μορφὰ βάλλει πόθον, ἢ πάλι μοῦσα,
> ἢ χάρις, ἢ...τί λέγω; πάντα· πυρὶ φλέγομαι.

1. Basse: an iambic poet: cf. Ov. *Trist.* IV, x, 47–8 *Ponticus heroo, Bassus quoque clarus iambis, dulcia conuictus membra fuere mei.*

5. Antiopae: Antiope was daughter of Nycteus and became mother by Jupiter (= Zeus) of Amphion and Zethus. It was this Amphion whose lyre bewitched the stones to build the wall of Thebes.

6. Hermionae: the daughter of Menelaus, whose hand was disputed by Neoptolemus and Orestes.

7. formosi temporis aetas: 'the age of beauty', or (giving a value to the combination of *aetas* and *temporis*) 'all the age of beauty', i.e. with an emphasis on duration. For *formosum tempus* = 'age of beauty', cf. Hor. *Epod.* XVI, 64 *tempus aureum* = 'age of gold', or Ov. *Met.* I, 89 *aurea...aetas.*

9–10. nedum...turpis eat: 'much less, if matched with common beauties, could she fail to win the judge's favour, and come away defeated and ashamed'. Propertius imagines a judgement like that of Paris. *duro* is said here from the loser's point of view.

10. inferior: 'defeated'.
turpis: 'humiliated' by her defeat.

11. extrema: as is shown by the contrast which follows, *extrema* here means 'least' (because 'last'). It is used somewhat similarly in Livy XXII, xxix, 8, where an order *of merit* is given by the series *primum...secundum...extremi ingenii (uirum)....*

13. ingenuus color: this may be (*a*) a 'natural complexion', not produced by cosmetics; cf. Juv. III, 20 *nec...ingenuum uiolarent marmora tofum*; or (*b*) a 'fair complexion'; cf. D. R. Shackleton Bailey, *Propertiana*, p. 16, where the author points out that in Cic. *Pis.* 1 the opposite, namely a *seruilis color*, is attributed to a person of swarthy complexion; or (*c*) ? a 'delicate complexion'; cf. Ov. *Am.* I, vii, 50 (*sustinui*)...*ingenuas ungue notare genas.*

13–14. et quae gaudia sub tacita dicere ueste libet: ?'and joys which I prefer (*libet*) to recite in secret'. Some think the text corrupt, but the rather strange form of expression may be Propertius' own. For the aposiopesis cf. I, xiii, 18 *et quae deinde meus celat, amice, pudor*. For *sub tacita ueste dicere* cf. II, xxv, 30 *in tacito cohibe gaudia clausa sinu*, and the phrase *in sinu gaudere* (Cic. *T.D.* III, 51; Seneca, *Ep.* cv, 3; Tib. III, xix, 8 = IV, xiii, 8) used of one who rejoices silently about his own good fortune. The *sinus* in these phrases is the deep fold of the toga across the breast. It thus seems possible that *sub tacita ueste dicere* means here in effect 'keep to oneself', as does *suo premit ore* at Virg. *Aen.* VII, 103; or perhaps 'tell in private'. But there can naturally be no certainty about this.

[Many editors read *ducere* and take *ueste* as referring to bed-clothes. But *libet*—'I am glad to', 'I choose to'—does not seem a strong enough verb to be then appropriate.]

16. hoc magis accepta fallit uterque fide: here *fallit* must mean 'defeats your efforts'. *accepta fide* would normally mean 'having received an assurance (from the other)'; cf. Liv. XXXVIII, xxxiii, 3 and XXXIX, xii, 4; also Ter. *Eun.* 139. It is commonly understood here as standing for *data acceptaque fide* and meaning 'as we have vowed to one another to do' or 'in accordance with our mutual pledges'.

17. non impune feres: cf. Cat. LXXVIII, 9 *uerum id non impune feres*; Ov. *Met.* II, 474 *haud impune feres....*

19–20. nec tibi me...committet...nec te quaeret: she will not let Propertius keep company any more with Bassus, and she will not visit or invite (*quaeret* could mean either) Bassus herself.

23–4. nullas...et...: the *et* may be justified by the fact that the thought in the hexameter, though negative in form, is positive in content: she will make her laments at *every* altar.

Cf. however also II, iv, 12 *huic nullum caeli tempus et aura nocet.*

24. et quicumque sacer qualis ubique lapis: 'every sort of sacred stone that anywhere there is'. The expression looks like a parody of the language of religious formulae, e.g. Liv. XXXVI, ii, 5 *quisquis magistratus eos ludos quando* (= *quandocumque*) *ubique* (= *ubicumque*) *faxit, hi ludi recte facti donaque data recte sunto.* For prayers addressed to sacred stones cf. Lucr. V, 1198–9 *nec pietas ullast uelatum saepe uideri uertier ad lapidem atque omnes accedere ad aras.*

26. sibi cum rapto cessat amore decus: 'when her charms lie idle because a love has been stolen from her'. For *cessare* in this sense cf. II, viii, 30 (Achilles) *cessare in tectis pertulit arma sua.* For *sibi* where *ei* would be more regular, cf. Sall. *Jug.* LXI *Metellus...in his urbibus quae ad se defecerant...praesidia imponit.* [*decus* is a correction for *deus* of the MSS.]

27. praecipue nostri = 'especially my love'. For *nostri* thus used cf. Tac. *Ann.* VI, 22 *initia nostri* = 'our beginnings'; Sen. *Ep.* LXI, 3 *finem nostri* = 'our end'. This genitive of the personal pronoun is much more commonly used when the genitive is objective, so that *amor nostri* would more usually mean 'love of me', which the context here excludes.

adoro: unlike the simple verb *oro*, the compound *adoro* is not found elsewhere with a verbal construction, but only with accusative of the person to whom prayer or worship is addressed. Cf. note on I, iii, 3.

V

See introductory note to the preceding elegy.

2. pares: 'the two of us together'; cf. Virg. *Georg.* III, 169 *iunge pares* = 'yoke in pairs'; *Aen.* IX, 182 *pariterque* (= together) *in bella ruebant.* The word *pares* cannot here mean 'well-matched' since it appears from lines 3–4, 19–23, 27–30, etc. that Propertius' relations with Cynthia are by no means harmonious.

3. meos...furores: 'a raging passion such as this of mine'.

5. et miser ignotos uestigia ferre per ignis: i.e. 'you are about to run into dangers of which you have no idea'. The image is probably from hot lava hidden under a layer of ash. Horace uses it at *Od.* II, i, 7 *incedis per ignes suppositos cineri doloso* with a somewhat different application, to indicate an enterprise in which a person must pick his way warily, though he may have been fully aware of its hazardous nature when undertaking it.

6. e tota toxica Thessalia: potions intended to cure or cause love, work of witches, for which Thessaly was famous.

7. similis collata: for this pleonasm cf. Varro, *L.L.* IX, 28 *non bos ad bouem collatus similis*.

8. molliter irasci non sciet illa tibi: here *sciet* is a conjecture for *solet*, which is the reading of the best MSS. *solet* could be construed only by taking *tibi* as an 'ethic' dative (= e.g. 'I'll have you know'), which does not seem possible in view of its position in the line *and* the sentence; an 'ethic' dative stands usually in an unemphatic position.

10. quanta: unusually, for *quot*; cf. Stat. *Silu.* IV, iii, 152.

11. non tibi...relinquet ocellos: 'will not leave you master of your own eyes'. Cf. I, ix, 27 *quippe ubi non liceat uacuos seducere ocellos*; Ov. *Am.* II, xix, 19 *tu quoque quae nostros rapuisti nuper ocellos*.

12. animis: (?) with *feros*, meaning 'pride' or 'spirit'; or (?) instrumental, with *alligat*, referring to Cynthia's imperious temper.

una: 'above all others', cf. II, iii, 29 *gloria Romanis una es tu nata puellis*; II, ix, 32 *hoc unum didicit femina semper opus*; and the fuller form of the expression at II, xxii, 45 *hic unus dolor est ex omnibus acer amanti*; Virg. *Aen.* III, 321 *o felix una ante alias Priameia uirgo*.

15. tremulus...orietur...horror: 'a trembling and a quaking will come over you'. For this sympton of love cf. the ode of Sappho quoted by the author *On the Sublime*, ch. x.

maestis...fletibus: ablative of attendant circumstances.

22. cur sim toto corpore nullus ego: cf. Plin. *N.H.* XI, 2 *in his tam paruis (corporibus) atque tam nullis*.

24. priscis...imaginibus: 'noble ancestry', here symbolized by the busts of bygone members of the family which stood (in the atrium) in the houses of the nobility and were carried in their funeral processions.

25. quod si parua tuae dederis uestigia culpae: this has been variously understood, as follows:

(*a*) 'but if you do not show enough signs of your passion'; cf. I, xviii, 17 *an quia parua damus mutato signa colore?* = 'or is it because I do not give evidence enough (of my love) by a

wan countenance (that Cynthia is angry with me)?' For *uestigia*
= *signa* cf. Ov. *A.A.* II, 331 *omnibus his inerunt gratae uestis ι
curae*. For *parua* = 'not sufficient' cf. I, xviii, 17 already
quoted, and III, v, 44 *Tityo iugera pauca nouem*, and Ov. *Her.*
XVIII, 114 *et querimur paruas noctibus esse moras*. For *culpa* in
the sense required for this rendering (*strong* or *abject* love, on
the part of a man) there seems to be no clear parallel; in IV, iv,
70 (*Vesta*) *culpam alit et plures condit in ossa faces* the reference
is to shameful love on the part of a woman, and *culpa* in the
case of men usually means infidelity to wife or mistress or has
the rather unemotional connotations of the English word
'adventure'. But there seems no reason why *culpa* should not
be used of a man's passion, as *errata* is in I, ix, 33 and *error* in
I, xiii, 35 and in Virg. *Ecl.* VIII, 41 *ut me malus abstulit error*.

(*b*) 'if you show even small signs of your old irregularities'.
This gives *culpa* one of its common meanings, for it appears
from I, xiii, 5 ff. that the man addressed was known as a roving
lover. Then for *parua* = 'even small...' cf. I, xix, 24 *flectitur
assiduis certa* (even a loyal) *puella minis*.

(*c*) '... by the least indiscretion you betray the fact that you are
having this affair'. An attachment to a courtesan that excited
notice was disgraceful; cf. Ter. *Andr.* 444-5 *amauit; tum id clam:
cauit ne unquam infamiae ea res sibi esset, ut uirum fortem decet*.

26. **rumor eris:** 'you will be a byword', i.e. a subject of
critical or derisive gossip. For *rumor* in this sense cf. the use of
fabula in Hor. *Epod.* XI, 7-8 *heu me, per urbem—nam pudet
tanti mali—fabula quanta fui*, and in Ov. *Am.* III, i, 21-2 *fabula—
nec sentis—tota iactaris in urbe, dum tua praeterito facta pudore
refers*. [In Pers. V, 152 *cinis et manes et fabula fies* the word
fabula seems to have a somewhat different meaning, 'just a
memory' or 'just a tale' as opposed to what is real or live or
solid.]

Why will he soon be a byword? It depends how we take line
25. If we take it in the third of the senses propounded in the
note on that line, he will be a byword because people will be
saying that the great Gallus is 'making a fool of himself' with
a woman. If we take line 25 in the first or second of the senses
propounded, we have to understand that Cynthia will express
her displeasure by telling tales about him (cf. I, iv, 21-2), or that
the plight he will be reduced to as a result of her displeasure will
attract comment (cf. II, xxiv, 5-6, I, xviii, *passim*, III, xxv, 1-2).

27. **tum**: there are two alternative ways of taking this. Either it refers to the situation anticipated in line 26; or it picks up again the *tum* of line 19.

31. **Galle**: we do not know anything about this Gallus, except from this poem and from x, xiii and xx, which are also addressed to him. He is not Cornelius Gallus or Aelius Gallus, for neither of them was of noble ancestry (cf. lines 23–4).

32. **uenit**: 'complies'. In erotic poetry *uenio* can be used as well of a woman who receives a lover as of one who goes to him.

VI

This elegy is in form the rejection of an invitation. In content it is a discourse on a theme (the contrast between the lover and the man of action) that is also propounded in Tibullus I, i, 53 ff.:

> te bellare decet terra, Messalla, marique,
>   ut domus hostiles praeferat exuuias;
> me retinent uinctum formosae uincla puellae,
>   et sedeo duras ianitor ante fores.
> non ego laudari curo, mea Delia; tecum
>   dummodo sim, quaeso, segnis inersque uocer.

* * *

> hic ego dux milesque bonus; uos, signa tubaeque,
>   ite procul: cupidis uulnera ferte uiris.

2. **Tulle**: nephew (see line 19) of L. Volcacius Tullus, who was consul 33 B.C. and proconsul of Asia 30–29 B.C. Poems i, xiv and xxii (the last) of this book are also addressed to Tullus.

ducere uela: 'set our sails'. In Plin. *N.H.* XIX, 23 *ducere uela* is used of drawing the awnings of an amphitheatre.

3. **Rhipaeos...montes**: legendary mountains to the north of Scythia.

4. **ulterius**: apparently used here by Propertius as a variant for *ultra* and so construed.

domos...Memnonias: Ethiopia.

6. **mutatoque graues saepe colore preces**: 'and insistent prayers made more touching by wan cheeks'. *saepe* can hardly go with *mutato* as frequent changes of colour are not appropriate to the situation; so it must go with *preces* and have a value similar to that of an adjective as *semper* has in I, xvi, 47 *semper*...

fletibus or *saepe* in I, iii, 44 *saepe...moras* (and cf. note on I, xxii, 2). *mutato colore* could possibly be an ablative absolute or of attendant circumstances, but if taken causally with *graues* it gives more value to that word. For *grauis* in the sense 'having weight' and so 'effective', 'moving', etc. cf. Plaut. *Trin.* 388 *grauius tuum erit unum uerbum ad eam rem quam centum mea.*

7. **argutat...ignis:** 'talks on and on about her love for me'. *arguto* is found also in Petronius, and the deponent form *argutor* in comedy; the meaning is given by Nonius, p. 245 *argutari dicitur loquaciter proloqui.*

9. **illa meam mihi iam se denegat:** 'already she is telling me that she is no longer mine'. She may mean that Propertius no longer loves her; in which case *mea* is to be understood as at I, viii, 26. Or she may be announcing (already, i.e. her reaction has been prompt) the withdrawal of her favours; in which case *mea* is used like *tua* in I, ix, 26; a similar sense can also be obtained by a somewhat different construction of the Latin— 'she is refusing herself to me'.

10. **ingrato...uiro:** 'an ungrateful lover', i.e. one who has become cool after receiving her kindness. [*ingrato* is a correction for *irato* of the MSS.]

12. **a pereat si quis lentus amare potest:** cf. II, xxiii, 12 *a pereant, si quos ianua clausa iuuat.* The imprecation here has lost its literal force and means roughly 'shame on' (anyone who can be a lover and yet cold-hearted). At I, xvii, 13 it is stronger and means 'a curse on...'.

15. **deducta...puppi:** when the ship has been launched but has not yet sailed, the time of farewells.

16. **ora:** comparison with Cynthia's behaviour elsewhere (e.g. III, viii, 6 and IV, viii, 64) makes it reasonably certain that the face which is in danger of getting scratched is that of Propertius; and the idea of the possessive *mea* is easily supplied from *mihi* in the previous line.

17. **osculaque opposito dicat sibi debita uento:** the imagined situation in prospect seems to be this: while the ship waits at anchor (as would be usual) for a favourable wind Propertius tries to comfort Cynthia with kisses, but she rebuffs him, saying that his proffered attentions are not due to love for her (else he would not be leaving her) but simply to the circumstances that delay his sailing; she has the wind to thank for them, not him. We are left to supply so much from imagination

because (one suspects) the idea is already familiar to the poet and his readers from past poetry; Cynthia will be carrying on 'in all the usual ways'. That the idea was already familiar is of course conjecture; that it was familiar afterwards we know from such passages as Ov. *Her.* VII, 43 (Dido) *quod tibi malueram sine me debere procellis*, and Valerius Fl. II, 407 (Hypsipyle) *ergo moras caelo cursumque tenentibus undis debuimus....* We can translate: 'and declare it is the adverse wind that she has to thank for my kisses'. With *oscula* supply *mea*, as with *ora* in the line before. *sibi debita* = 'owed by her', *sibi* being dative of agent after the past participle.

19. tu patrui meritas conare anteire securis: i.e. do you make ready to precede your uncle, whose well-earned honour it will be to govern that province. For *conor* = ' be about to ', 'prepare to', etc. cf. Ter. *Phorm.* 52 *at ego obuiam conabar tibi*; Ter. *Heaut.* 240 *dum moliuntur, dum conantur annus est*; Cic. *Fam.* v, xii, 1 *coram me tecum eadem haec agere saepe conantem deterruit pudor quidam*; also in this book I, iii, 12. The word *secures* indicates the lictors attending the proconsul in his province. For *meritas* = ' deserved ' cf. Cic. *Phil.* VII, 10 *meritos ... honores* (conferred by the senate on Octavian).

anteire might mean either that he is to travel to Asia ahead of the proconsul or that he will march ahead of him as part of a military escort or walk ahead of him as a member of his suite. For the general idea involved in the last of these possible meanings cf. Ov. *Ex Pont.* IV, ix, 18 *consulis ante pedes ire iuberer eques*, where however the situation is a special one.

[Some think that *patrui...anteire secures* here means 'outdo your uncle's proconsulship'. If so, the uncle's proconsulship is already past and Tullus is going to Asia in some other context, unknown to us. But a friend of Propertius at this time is likely to have been a young man, no rival yet for a proconsul. And line 34 is most easily understood as meaning that Tullus will be a member of the proconsul's staff. See also note on p. 102.]

20. uetera...iura refer: this might mean either 'restore rights' or (perhaps) 'bring back law [and order] as before'. In any case, the new regime is supposed to be an improvement on that of Antony.

21. cessauit amori: 'had leisure for love', *cessare* being here used as synonym for *uacare* and construed accordingly.

26. hanc animam extremae reddere nequitiae: 'yield up

my life to utter profligacy', i.e. bring myself through profligacy to an early death; cf. Val. Max. III, v, 3 *foedae ac sordidae intemperantiae spiritum reddidit.*

32. arata: a term used for ploughland in technical prose. Here it may stand, by an extension of meaning, for land in general; or the poet may really have in mind the picture of a river flowing between cultivated fields.

33. carpere...ibis: for this poetic infinitive of purpose or result after a verb of motion cf. I, i, 12 and note, I, xi, 5, I, xx, 24.

34. accepti pars eris imperii: for *acceptus* = 'beloved' or 'popular' cf. II, ix, 43 *te nihil in uita nobis acceptius;* Liv. I, xv, 8 (*Romulus*)...*longe ante alios acceptissimus militum animis;* these instances have all the attached dative; but in Tac. *Ann.* XV, 43 certain measures adopted by Nero after the fire of Rome are described simply as *accepta,* i.e. 'welcome' or 'popular'. By *pars eris* is meant that Tullus will be a member of the staff of this popular governor.

36. duro sidere: 'under an unkind star'. It is his fate to be tormented by unhappy love.

VII

This elegy forms a pair with Elegy ix. Both are addressed to Ponticus, an epic poet (i.e., according to ancient ideas, a poet in by far the grandest and best department of poetry), who is here warned that he may fall in love, and in Elegy ix will be found to have done so. Both pieces involve a comparison between elegy and other forms of poetry, and an assertion of its peculiar value to lovers. Similar thoughts occur in Tibullus II, iv, 15 ff.:

> ite procul, Musae, si non prodestis amanti;
> non ego uos, ut sint bella canenda, colo;
> nec refero solisque uias et qualis, ubi orbem
> compleuit, uersis luna recurrit equis.
> ad dominam faciles aditus per carmina quaero;
> ite procul, Musae, si nihil ista ualent.

1. Pontice: an epic poet; cf. on I, iv, 1. Poem ix also is addressed to him.

2. fraternae...militiae: the war between the brothers Eteocles and Polynices. Ponticus was writing a Thebaid.

3. ita sim felix: 'as I hope to be happy'. The prayer is a conventional formula giving positiveness to an assertion. It has a value similar to that of 'I vow' or 'I'll swear' in English. Here it may have an affectionately ironical tone.

5. consuemus: probably a contracted form of *consueuimus*.

agitamus: 'are occupied with'; cf. *agitare conuiuia*, etc.

6. aliquid duram...in dominam: 'some means to soften the hard heart of my lady'.

7. nec tantum...dolori: i.e. and write not as a poet would but as a lover must.

8. aetatis tempora dura: 'the trials I endure, day in, day out'.

9. uitae modus: 'my life's span'.

11–12. me laudent...minas: 'may people tell in praise of me how a girl of talent chose me above all others for her lover; and tell too how often I bore her anger, undeserved'. The 3rd person plural in *laudent* is as in English 'they say...', 'people will say...', etc. and Latin *ferunt, dicunt*, etc.; cf. II, xx, 9 *mi licet aeratis astringant bracchia nodis*, etc.

solum need not suggest that she literally had no other lover, for cf. Ov. *A.A.* I, 131 *Romule, militibus scisti dare commoda solus!*

For *minas* cf. on I, x, 26 and I, xix, 24.

11. laudent...placuisse: an unusual construction with *laudo*, but cf. Virg. *Aen.* II, 585 *exstinxisse nefas...laudabor*.

15. concusserit: we should expect *percusserit*; just as in III, xvi, 16 *percutit ante faces* we should expect *concutit*. This avoidance of the obvious compound is worth noting as a mannerism of Propertius; see note on I, iii, 3. But it remains possible that *concusserit* here is meant to convey the force of a shot that makes the victim reel.

16. (quod nolim nostros, heu, uoluisse deos): '(and I hope, ah I hope, that our gods may not so decree)'. For the sentiment cf. I, vi, 23 *et tibi non unquam nostros puer iste labores afferat*. For the form of expression cf. Virg. *Aen.* V, 50 *sic di uoluistis*; also Ov. *Fast.* IV, 122 *a, nolim uictas hoc meminisse deas!* For *heu* giving pathos to a wish for the future cf. II, xx, 16 *si fallo, cinis, heu, sit mihi uterque grauis*. For the infinitive *uoluisse* without perfect force cf. on I, i, 15, etc. For *nostros...deos* of the lover's gods cf. II, xxxiv, 26.

[The reading printed in the text and translated above is a conjectured substitute for *euiolasse* of the MSS. In four other places in Propertius our principal manuscripts give *e* or *et* where it cannot possibly be right. See I, xix, 22 (*ne te*)... *abstrahat* e *nostro puluere iniquus amor*; II, xii, 15 *euolat* e *nostro quoniam de pectore nusquam*...; II, xxii, 44 *quid iuuat* et *nullo ponere uerba loco?*; IV, x, 27 E (*or* Et) *Veii ueteres, et uos tùm regna fuistis*. ... In all of these *heu* suits, and here too.

Exclamatory *ei* might at first sight seem preferable to *heu* in these passages as nearer to the MSS. Though it appears to be confined in extant classical Latin (at least after Catullus) to the phrase *ei mihi*, it occurs quite often in Plautus and Terence (and cf. also Cat. LXVIII, 92–3) without the attached *mihi*, and Propertius' language shows some affinities with theirs. But where it occurs it seems always to stand as first word and never in parenthesis.

Alternatively, *a* might be read in all these passages; as preposition in I, xix, 22, and as an exclamation in the rest.]

   17. longe: i.e. of no avail to you: cf. Virg. *Aen*. XII, 52 *longe illi dea mater erit*; Caes. *B.G*. I, 36 (Ariovistus threatening the Aedui) *si id non fecissent, longe his fraternum nomen populi Romani afuturum*.

   agmina septem: those of the Seven Champions who supported Polynices; cf. on 2 above.

   18. surda: 'unhearing', and so of no help to you; and also 'unheard' and so 'forgotten'.

   23. nec poterunt...sepulcro: perhaps we are to supply something here, e.g. 'you will believe that...'; as in II, iii, 37 *nunc, Pari, tu sapiens et tu, Menelae, fuisti*, where we supply, 'I agree that...'

VIIIA

An appeal to Cynthia not to leave Propertius and go overseas with another admirer. Its counterpart in the present collection seems to be Elegy xi, in which Cynthia is absent (at Baiae) and Propertius appeals to her to be faithful to him while she is there and to come back to him as quickly as possible.

What Cynthia is proposing to do in this elegy is what Lycoris in Virgil's tenth *Eclogue* (see *Ecl*. x, 22–3 and 45–9) is represented as having done already. The Servian commentary on Virgil says that *Ecl*. x, 45–9 is full of echoes from the works of Cornelius Gallus, to whom *Ecl*. x is addressed, and who was also first of the series of Latin love elegists. It may be that in this elegy of Propertius there are reminiscences of Gallus' poems, or of a particular poem of his on a similar subject.

1. **mea cura**: probably 'my love for you'. But it could alternatively mean 'your love for me': cf. the meaning of *tua cura* at I, xv, 31.

3. **quicumque est, iste**: here *quicumque est* is a conventional formula that gives a tone of intentional contempt to the sentence. It indicates ostentatiously that the man's name is of no consequence. A fair translation here would be 'this person (*quicumque est*), this friend of yours (*iste*)'.

[The corresponding phrase in Ov. *Am.* III, ii, 21 means 'you, there!'; in Ov. *R.A.* 366 it means 'a certain obscure (Zoilus)'. But of course it may also be used without any suggestion of contempt.]

4. **uento quolibet ire**: 'to sail in any weather' (*quolibet* must go with *uento* because *uento* without it would lack point).

7. **fulcire pruinas** : see addendum on p. 102.

9–20. 'May the length of winter be doubled and the rising of the Pleiads be delayed, so that the sailors are kept inactive and your ship's moorings cannot be cast off from the Tyrrhene shore or the unkind breeze bear away my prayers unheeded. Nevertheless (*atque*; cf. L.S. IV 8) may I see no such wintry season's storms when your ship *has* sailed and is out at sea, though (*ut*) it leave me rooted on the empty beach, shaking my fist and calling you cruel, cruel. No, rather I pray (*sed*, answering *non* in 13), despite your treatment of me, traitress, that Galatea may be propitious to your voyage: be safely rowed past the Ceraunian cliffs, and may Oricos receive you in the quiet waters of its harbour'.

For the free use of *uideo* in line 13 cf. II, xvi, 49 *uidistis toto sonitus percurrere caelo*. For the sense of *tali sub sidere uentos* in the same line cf. Virg. *Aen.* IV, 309 *hiberno moliris sidere classem*, and *Catalepton* IX, 47 *trucem aduerso perlabi sidere pontum*. For the object required to be understood after the transitive verb in line 20 cf. II, xxiv, 49 *noli nobilibus, noli conferre beatis....*

[The text translated above differs from the best MS. tradition by reading *tali sub sidere* for *talis subsidere* in 13; *ut* for *et* in 15; and *utere*[1] for *ut te* in 19.]

---

[1] Löfstedt in *Syntactica* I (1928), p. 80 argues that *ut te* in line 19 snould not be altered, and that *praeuecta* stands nevertheless as a vocative, by a

10. Vergiliis: the Pleiades, whose rising in the spring marked the beginning of the sailing season.

11. Tyrrhena: at this date the port of departure would probably be Puteoli; the epithet *Tyrrhenus* is applied to the sea off that port by Virgil at *Georg.* II, 164. It may seem odd, especially after line 5, that Cynthia should be supposed to go by sea all around the coast of Italy from Puteoli to Brundisium, when she could perfectly well go overland. From Brundisium to Oricos (line 20) she will have to go by sea anyway.

18. Galatea: a Nereid.

19. Ceraunia: mountains on the coast of Epirus, including the dangerous promontory Acroceraunia.

20. Oricos: a port near Acroceraunia.

22. uera querar: 'utter my just complaint'; cf. Silius Ital. VII, 738 *si fas uera queri*, and the sense of *uerus* in Virg. *Aen.* XII, 694 *me uerius unum pro vobis foedus luere*....

[*uera* is a conjecture for *uerba* of the MSS.]

23. nec me deficiet nautas rogitare citatos: 'I shall not cease to...'. This construction of *deficio* (impersonal, apparently, or with infinitive for subject) seems not to occur elsewhere in classical Latin.

citatos: cf. Ov. *Her.* VII, 101 *hinc ego me sensi noto quater ore citari* ('I heard a voice calling me').

25–6. Atraciis...Hylaeis: Atrax was the name of a town in Thessaly, and of a river in Aetolia. The Hylaei were a people supposed to live beyond Scythia. (There was also a people in Illyria called Hylleis.) It is uncertain whether the names have been correctly transmitted. The general sense is clear and sure enough: Cynthia wherever she is will still be Propertius' love.

VIII B

Our MSS. mark no division at line 27, but modern editions usually do so, because Propertius here begins to talk about Cynthia in the third person, after addressing her in the second person in lines 1–26. What we have in lines 27–46 is evidently meant as a pendant to what has gone before.

29. falsa: 'mistaken', or 'disappointed'.

32. sine me dulcia regna negat: 'declares that without me a king's riches would not give her joy'. This is a good example peculiar syntactical licence. Though I have adopted *utere* to obtain a regular construction, I expect some readers will want to study what Löfstedt has to say. He applies it also to I, xi, 9. It might perhaps be relevant to I, xix, 18 as well.

of compressed expression, involving (a) a heavy emphasis on
regna, and (b) ellipsis of the verbal syntax appropriate to a
'remote future condition in *oratio obliqua*'.

**34–5. et quocumque modo maluit esse mea quam sibi
dotatae regnum uetus Hippodamiae**: the status of *sibi* is
illustrated by the full construction shown in Tib. II, ii, 13 ff.
*nec tibi malueris totum quaecumque per orbem fortis arat ualido
rusticus arua boue, nec tibi gemmarum quidquid felicibus Indis
nascitur, Eoi qua maris unda rubet.*

36. quas Elis opes ante pararat equis: the reference
evidently is to winnings accumulated before the coming of
Pelops; they would have contributed to increase the riches of
the kingdom that was Hippodamia's 'dower' (see note on I, ii,
19–20), and they may have consisted in the proceeds of Oenomaus' victories over unsuccessful suitors. [The form of the
expression *ante pararat* may have been suggested by common
phrases such as *ante parta praeda, laus*, etc., *ante parta bona,
decora*, etc.]

37. quamuis magna daret. . . : the subject is the rival mentioned in viii A, 3.

39–40. hanc ego non auro. . .obsequio: this means simply
that his success was achieved, not with gold and jewels, but with
poetry. It does not mean that he tried and failed with gold and
jewels before succeeding with poetry.

**41–2. sunt igitur Musae, neque amanti tardus Apollo, quis
ego fretus amo: Cynthia rara mea est**: 'and so the powers in
whom I put my trust as a lover have not failed me; the Muses
are goddesses indeed, and Apollo is not slow to come to a lover's
aid; for see, the incomparable Cynthia is mine!'

46. ista meam norit gloria canitiem: 'that glory shall
know my old age' is put by a 'figure' instead of the more
obvious 'my old age shall know that glory'; cf. Mart. XIV, xliii, 2
non norat parcos uncta lucerna patres.

IX

See introductory note to Elegy vii.

3. uenis ad iura: 'make your submission to'. Cf. Ov. *Am.*
I, ii, 20 *porrigimus uictas ad tua iura manus.*

4. quaeuis: in its normal use *quaeuis* would mean 'any girl
at all', as at 14 below. Here (with less emphasis on the idea that
the choice is indifferent) it means 'some girl'; cf. Lucr. I, 102–3

*tutemet a nobis iam quouis tempore uatum terriloquis uictus dictis
desciscere quaeres*; Prop. II, xiii, 43–4 *atque utinam primis animam
me ponere cunis iussisset quaeuis de tribus una soror*; Hor. *Sat.* I, iii,
64–5 *simpliciter quis…ut forte legentem aut tacitum impellat*
(*impediat* Bentley) *quouis sermone molestus.*

5. non me…uincant…dicere: here *non…uincant* means
in effect 'would not be better able…', and the infinitive
dicere is governed by that meaning.

Chaoniae…columbae: the prophetic doves of the oracle
of Dodona in Epirus. Chaonia was a region of Epirus.

in amore: 'in a matter of love', 'on the subject of love'.

10. Amphioniae moenia…lyrae: the walls of Thebes:
see note on I, iv, 5.

11. Mimnermus was an elegiac poet of Colophon who lived
in the seventh century B.C.

13. compone: 'put away'; cf. Liv. XXXVI, xliv, 2 *armamenta
componens* ('stowing away the tackle'); Hor. *Od.* IV, xiv, 52
te…Sygambri compositis uenerantur armis ('their arms laid
aside').

20. infernae rotae: Ixion's wheel.

23–4. nullus amor cuiquam facilis ita praebuit alas ut
non alterna presserit ille manu: perhaps 'never does love
grant any lover so smooth a course that he does not check it too
from time to time'; but we cannot be certain what image is
intended. For *nullus* used adverbially and meaning 'not' or
'never' cf. Cic. *Att.* XI, xxiv, 4 *Philotimus…nullus uenit.* For
the meaning above proposed for *facilis* and *pressit* cf. Virg.
Georg. I, 40 *da facilem cursum…*; Cic. *Brut.* 332 *cursum ingenii
tui, Brute, premit haec importuna clades ciuitatis*; Virg. *Aen.* I, 63
et premere et laxas…dare iussus habenas. For *alterna manu* of
an intermittent action of the hand, instead of (as in some other
passages)|a hand-over-hand action, cf. the sense of the adjective
in Virg. *Aen.* XII, 386 *alternos…nitentem cuspide gressus*;
Sil. It. VI, 361 *qui uoce alternos nautarum temperat ictus.* It
seems that *alas* stands virtually for *cursum* and that Propertius
has transferred the wings that we normally associate with the
love-god who is subject of the sentence to the lover whose
experience he controls. [The form of the sentence may also
have been influenced by unconscious reminiscence of phrases
such as *faciles aurem praebere* (II, xxi, 15), *facili…aure* (I, i, 31),
etc.] See also Addenda, p. 102.

26. acrius illa subit...si qua tua est: 'the wound a woman deals is sharper still, if she is all your own.' For this sense of *subit* cf. Lucan, I, 210–11 *si...subeant uenabula pectus.*

28. alio nomine: 'for any other woman's sake'; literally 'on any other account'; cf. Cic. *Fin.* II, 21 *qui cum luxuriose uiuerent...non reprehenderentur eo nomine....*

cedat (here) = *concedat* = *permittat.*

29. manus: 'his stroke'.

30. a fuge: a correction for *aufuge* of the MSS., made because *aufugio* seems always to be intransitive.

32. nedum: in Ciceronian prose *nedum* is used always after negative or quasi-negative propositions and so is to be translated 'still less'. Later, as here and in Liv. IX, 18 *adulationes etiam uictis Macedonibus graues, nedum uictoribus,* it may occur after a positive proposition and then has to be translated 'still more'. [It will be noticed that both in the Livian passage and here the essential meaning can very easily be cast in a negative form: 'the Macedonians would not have liked...still less did they...'; 'rocks and stones would not be proof against...still less is it likely that you can be.']

possint...possis: note that *possum* in both lines has not its full value as an independent verb, but only supplies the value of a potential subjunctive to *cedere.*

spiritus iste leuis: 'frail creature that you are'. At III, xviii, 10 *spiritus* means 'soul' or 'ghost'. Here it seems to mean 'creature that breathes'.

33. si pudor est: cf. Virg. *Ecl.* VII, 44 *ite domum pasti, si quis pudor, ite iuuenci*; Ov. *Am.* III, ii, 23–4 *tua contrahe crura, si pudor est, rigido nec preme terga genu.* The phrase has lost much of its literal force and may do no more than give a somewhat peremptory tone to a request: 'Come on now...', 'For goodness sake...'.

errata = *error* I, xiii, 35 = 'love'; cf. Virg. *Ecl.* VIII, 41 *ut uidi, ut perii, ut me malus abstulit error.*

34. quo pereas: 'the object (or occasion) of your passion'.

X

This elegy forms a pair with Elegy xiii. Both are addressed to the Gallus who has appeared earlier, in Elegy v, as an unwelcome candidate for Cynthia's favours. Both depict a situation similar to that of Catullus XLV, in which the poet is witness of a friend's amour.

In lines 15–30 here Propertius assumes a role similar to that assumed by Priapus in Tib. I, iv, 77–8:

> gloria cuique sua est: me qui spernentur amantes
> consultent; cunctis ianua nostra patet...

(see too 39 ff. in the same poem:

> cedas: obsequio plurima uincit amor...).

1. quies: by an extension of meaning = 'night'.

2. uestris...lacrimis: for pain and tears in connexion with a happy love cf. I, xiii, 15–16 *uidi ego te...flere iniectis, Galle, diu manibus*; II, xv, 35 *nostros...dolores*; ·III, viii, 23 *aut in amore dolere uolo aut audire dolentem, siue meas lacrimas siue uidere tuas.*

3. o noctem meminisse mihi iucunda uoluptas: there seems here to be a telescoping of two constructions: (a) *o noctem quam meminisse est iucunda uoluptas*, and (b) *o iucunda uoluptas meminisse noctem illam.*

5–6. cum te complexa morientem, Galle, puella uidimus et longa ducere uerba mora: 'with your mistress in your arms, swooning, and murmuring long-drawn words of love'.

5. complexa may be active (with *te* supplied as object), or (more probably) passive like *expertae* in I, iii, 18.

8. ruberet: probably here meaning no more than 'shone brightly'; cf. Hor. *Od.* II, xi, 9–10 *non semper...uno luna rubens nitet uultu* (whereas in Virg. *Georg.* I, 431 *uento semper rubet aurea Phoebe* the word denotes colour).

mediis caelo...equis: 'with her chariot in mid sky', cf. Ov. *Met.* x, 144 *in...concilio medius*, etc. Propertius has in mind the *full* moon, which is about half-way across the sky in the middle of the night.

11. concredere: 'confide in me', 'trust me with your secret'; cf. Plaut. *Cas.* 478 *ei ego amorem omnem meum concredui*; *Asin.* 80 *praesertim quom is me dignum quoi concrederet habuit*; see also 12–13 below. [The MS. tradition has *concedere* which would mean 'indulge'; cf. Ter. *Hec.* 244 *faciam ut tibi concedam neque tuae libidini aduersabor.*]

12. commissae munera laetitiae: 'reward for allowing me to witness your happiness'. For *munus* in this (extended) sense cf. Virg. *Aen.* VIII, 273 *tantarum in munere laudum.*

15. diuersos: 'parted'.

17. curas...recentis: the idea is of the pain of a wound, harder to cure because the wound is recent.

19–20. Cynthia me docuit semper quaecumque petenda quaeque cauenda forent: the phrasing suggests a doctor's instructions to his patient for the good of his health. The *quaecumque* clause gives the content of Cynthia's instructions. For the subjunctive in such a clause cf. Suet. *Aug.* XLIX, 2 *quicquid ...ubique militum esset...astrinxit.*

23. petiit: on the scansion see Platnauer, L. E. V., pp. 59–61.

24. pro uano...cadant: 'be spoken in vain and fall unheeded'. For *cado* in a similar sense cf. I, xvi, 34 and I, xvii, 4. The *uerba benigna* are such expressions of affection as the lady may utter when she is in a good mood. *tibi* is an ethic dative.

26. minas: this means of course literally 'threats', but here it seems to be used in an extended sense and to mean 'anger', of which threats are one manifestation. For another (different) extension of the meaning of *minae* cf. note on I, xix, 24 *flectitur assiduis certa puella minis.*

28. fruare: potential subjunctive: 'you are likely to...'.

29–30. is...erit: i.e. a man can expect to be happy with a mistress (i.e. in a single attachment) only by being her constant and devoted slave.

XI

See introductory note to Elegy viii, to which this poem seems to be a counterpart.

1. mediis...Baiis: 'amid the pleasures of Baiae'. Cf. Seneca, *Vit. Beat.* xxvi, 1 *sapiens tunc maxime paupertatem meditatur cum in mediis diuitiis constitit.* Because of the place's reputation, its name carries a connotation of luxury, pleasures, temptations, etc. Baiae was a fashionable resort in the northwest corner of the gulf of Naples, between the Lucrine lake and the promontory of Misenum.

2. Herculeis semita litoribus: 'the way along the shore that Hercules made'. Though *Herculeis* is attached grammatically to *litoribus*, it belongs in sense to *semita*; for the causeway in question (described by Strabo v, iv, 6) was legendarily supposed to have been built by Hercules. It ran along the strip of land which separates the Lucrine lake from the sea.

3–4. et modo Thesproti mirantem subdita regno proxima Misenis aequora nobilibus: 'and beholding with wonder how the sea near famed Miseni has lately been brought under Thesprotus' sway (or, added to Thesprotus' realm)'. In *Thesproti regno* there is presumably a reference to lake Avernus; cf. Hyginus, *Fab.* 88 *Thyestes scelere nefario cognito profugit ad regem Thesprotum, ubi lacus Auernus dicitur esse.* This sufficiently establishes the probability that *Thesproti regnum* in our present passage means lake Avernus. But something remains unexplained, for the Thesprotus and Avernus mentioned by Hyginus must have been Greek, whereas Propertius is speaking of Italy. The explanation may lie in some piece of mythology now lost to us, or in a belief (for several examples see Strabo VI, ii, 4 on Arethusa) in under-sea connexion between waters of the same name in different countries. The passage as a whole seems to refer to the making by Agrippa in 37 B.C. of the Portus Iulius. This involved connecting the Lucrine lake with the sea on the one hand and lake Avernus on the other, and the consequent *admission of the sea to Avernus* is what is dwelt on in other poetic descriptions; cf. III, xviii, 1 *clausus ab umbroso qua ludit pontus Auerno*; Virg. *Georg.* II, 164 *Tyrrhenusque fretis immittitur aestus Auernis.*

4. Misenis: on the coast between Baiae and the tip of the promontory of Misenum was a small town or village called variously by ancient authors Misenum (Pliny, *N.H.*) or Miseni (Plutarch, Josephus, etc.). The plural here is for the metre.

5. (ecquid te) nostri cura subit memores, a, ducere noctes: 'do you think of me? do you lie awake at night (alone) remembering me?'. For the construction cf. Virg. *Aen.* ix, 757–8 *si...uictorem ea cura subisset, rumpere claustra manu...* But I think here two ideas are combined: (1) *ecquid te cura subit nostri?*; and (2) *an tibi curae est memores nostri ducere noctes?* Also relevant is *cura* = 'love', and the special sense of *noctem ducere* exemplified in Plaut. *Truc.* 49 (*amator*) *si raras noctes ducit, ab animo perit.* [The MSS. give *adducere* here.]

6. in extremo...amore locus: 'room on the edge of your affections': cf. such expressions as *in extremo toro*, etc.; or 'some humble place in your affections'; cf. Ov. *Fast.* v, 22 *et Themis extremo saepe recepta loco est* (where the context shows that a lack of respect is meant).

8. e nostris carminibus: presumably 'from your place in

my poems'. This involves a jump in thought, for he means of course 'steal you from my embraces (so that I no longer have you for my inspiration)'. For such jumps cf. notes on I, i, 31 and I, vii, 23.

11. Teuthrantis: this is a correction for a word of improbable form in the MSS. Teuthras is known to us as (*a*) the name of a legendary Mysian king, and (*b*) the name of an inhabitant of (Italian) Cumae introduced by Silius Ital. (XI, 288). The connecting circumstance is that Italian Cumae (near Baiae) was originally founded by settlers from Aeolian Cumae, which was in Mysia. Evidently *Teuthrantis in unda* designates some lake or pool in the vicinity of Baiae. The duplication *in unda...lympha* is worth noticing as a point of Propertian style.

12. facilis cedere: this type of infinitive after an adjective that contains the idea 'ability to...', 'willingness to...', 'determination to...', etc., is quite common in the Augustan poets.

manu: an alternative form of the dative that is used elsewhere by Propertius, and by Virgil too.

14. compositam: after *uacet* we might expect the dative. But cf. *licet*, which is variously construed with dative and infinitive, with accusative and infinitive subject clause, and with a mixture as in Cic. *Balb.* 29 *si ciui Romano licet esse Gaditanum*....

15. amoto...custode: this is a correction for *amota* of the MSS. From 17–18 it is clear that the statement in 15–16 does not refer to Cynthia and so must be a general one. As such it requires the masculine *amoto*, for we seldom if ever hear of a duenna but frequently of a male in the office of *custos*.

16. communis deos: i.e. the gods by whom the two lovers have sworn to be true to one another.

17. non quia...non es...: in classical Latin *non quia* requires the *subjunctive* when what is stated in the clause following is said to be untrue, as here. But an exception none the less is found in Lucr. II, 3 *non quia uexari quemquamst iucunda uoluptas.* In silver Latin the use of the indicative in such cases becomes more common. [When what is stated in the clause following is not said to be untrue but is only rejected as an operative reason the indicative is normal in all periods.]

fama: 'honour'. The result (*fama*) is here put for the virtue (*fides* or *pudicitia*) that produces it. Cf. the meanings of 'honour' in English, and Publilius, B27 *bona fama in tenebris proprium splendorem tenet.*

18. sed quod in hac omnis parte timetur amor: 'but because at Baiae love (or Love) is always a menace'. For *hac in parte* = 'here' cf. Ov. *Met.* XIV, 398 *clamato...nequiquam Pico nullaque in parte reperto*; Hor. *Od.* III, iii, 39 *qualibet exules in parte regnanto beati*; Plin. *N.H.* II, v, 14 *quisquis est deus, si modo est aliquis, et quacumque in parte...*; Ter. *Heaut.* 57 *quod ego in propinqua parte* (next to) *amicitiae puto*; Silius Ital. IX, 271 *at campi in medio—namque hac in parte uidebat stare ducem Libyae....* For *hic* used of what is remote in space from the speaker because it is present in his thought cf. II, ix, 23–4 (even more clearly in line 26 of the same passage) and III, xxiii, 3–7, and Hor. *Epod.* XVI, 49 and 57. For *amor* symbolizing a rival's attentions and viewed as a danger to the lover cf. II, vi, 22 *per te nunc Romae quidlibet audet amor*, II, xxxiv, 1 *cur quisquam faciem dominae iam credat amori?* For *omnis* used adverbially to generalize a statement cf. (*a*) the corresponding adverbial use of *nullus*; e.g. I, ix, 23 *nullus amor cuiquam faciles ita praebuit alas...*; (*b*) such sentences as Ov. *R.A.* 95 *uerba dat omnis amor reperitque alimenta morando*, 462 *successore nouo uincitur omnis amor*; Prop. IV, ii, 9 *omnis amor magnus, sed aperto in coniuge maior*.

See also Addenda, p. 102.

21. an mihi nunc maior carae custodia matris?: 'would I guard more anxiously my own dear mother?'; cf. Plaut. *Truc.* 622 *quam mage amo quam matrem meam*; also here 23. [*nunc* in line 21 is a conjecture for *non* of the MS., recommended both by the sense obtained from it, and by Propertius' fondness for similar phrases: cf. I, ii, 25 *non ego nunc...* (and also at I, vi, 1 and I, xix, 1); II, iii, 33 *hac ego nunc...?*]

29. litora quae fuerunt castis inimica puellis: *fuerunt* is a correction for *fuerant* of the MSS. The context requires a general statement about Baiae, and does not admit a statement relating specifically to the past, which is what the *fuerant* of the MSS. would give. For the perfect giving a general statement based on experience cf. Virg. *Georg.* I, 160–1 *dicendum et quae sint duris agrestibus arma, quis sine nec potuere seri nec surgere messes*, etc.

castis...puellis: not necessarily or even probably 're-spectable young women', but courtesans who like Cynthia owe fidelity to a particular man. Cf. on I, i, 5.

30. crimen amoris: 'that bring reproach on love'; cf. Virg. *Aen.* X, 188 *crimen, Amor, uestrum* where the meaning must be the same.

XII

All our MSS. (except the second hands of *N* and *P*) make this elegy one with Elegy xi. It seems in fact to be a pendant to xi, as viii A is to viii B. Whereas in xi Cynthia was addressed, here the poet speaks to an unidentified third person, presumably imaginary.

1. desidiae: cf. III, xi, 1–4 *quid mirare, meam si uersat femina uitam et trahit addictum sub sua iura uirum, criminaque ignaui capitis mihi turpia fingis quod nequeam fracto rumpere uincla iugo?*

2. quod faciat nobis. . .Roma moram: 'because I stay in Rome', i.e. making love, instead of going on tours abroad, on foreign service, etc. (cf. I, vi). For *moram facere* = 'detain' cf. Virg. *Ecl.* x, 11–12 *nam neque Parnasi uobis iuga, nam neque Pindi ulla moram fecere.*

conscia: perhaps 'where my shame is known', the circumstance making Propertius' *desidia* more reprehensible; cf. Hor. *Epod.* xi, 7–8 *heu me, per urbem—nam pudet tanti mali—fabula quanta fui.* The word *conscius* is commonly used of sympathizers, abettors, etc., but in Ov. *Met.* II, 438 the *conscia silua* is witness of the speaker's shame; cf. also Cic. *Verr.* IV, 124.

3. What follows does not of course really answer the charge of *desidia* complained of in lines 1–2. What that charge has provoked is not a self-defence, but an outburst of self-pity. It has acted as an irritant.

4. Hypanis: the Bug, flowing into the Black Sea.
Eridanus: the Po.

8. simili. . .fide: it is not clear how this should be taken. The general sense required by the context is that Propertius' love for Cynthia was formerly requited. This can be arrived at in several ways, but none of them is easy. Thus (*a*) 'to be able to love so devotedly', with an emphasis on '*be able*', the idea being that what enabled him was Cynthia's reciprocal devotion to him; cf. the sentiment of line 5 above. (*b*) 'to love with such devotion for reward (*or* encouragement)'; *fide* being a loosely used ablative of attendant circumstances, as in III, xxii, 13–14 *Argoa natat inter saxa columba. . .(pinus)* 'sails between the (clashing) rocks with Argo's dove for guide'. (*c*) 'to love and feel so sure of his beloved'; for though *fides* does not usually stand for *fiducia* it does appear to do so at Virg. *Aen.* IX, 260–1 *quaecumque mihi fortuna fidesque est in uestris pono gremiis.*

9. num me deus obruit?: 'was it some god that crushed me?' [*num* is a necessary reading. The *non* given by the normally more authoritative MSS. would (like *nonne*) invite the assent of the reader; but a note of uncertainty is what is required.]

10. Prometheis iugis: the Caucasus, where Prometheus was chained.

diuidit: 'makes lovers cease to love'.

fueram: see on I, iii, 17.

11. mutat uia longa puellas: if, as is probable, this elegy is a pendant to xi, the reference here must be to Cynthia's trip to Baiae, from which we are to understand that she has come back with a changed attitude towards Propertius. *longa* has no emphasis on it, for cf. *exiguo tempore* in the next line.

13. longas solus cognoscere noctes: 'to experience long nights alone'.

16. aspersis gaudet…lacrimis: 'delights to be bedewed with tears'; literally 'delights when tears are sprinkled on him'. *aspergo* is used with accusative either (as here) of the liquid sprinkled or of the object besprinkled. For the idea cf. Lucan II, 30 *lacrimis sparsere deos* (women praying in temples).

XIII

See introductory note to Elegy x.

2. uacem: 'am left forlorn'. *uacare* is used absolutely of land without a master and so suits a poet without a mistress.

6. certus et in nullo quaeris amore moram: 'and purposely (*or*, steadfastly) avoid any lasting attachment'.

Alternatively there may be a construction ἀπὸ κοινοῦ: 'and never constant in any love (*in nullo amore certus*) you never seek to abide in any (*in nullo amore quaeris moram*)'.

7–8. perditus in quadam tardis pallescere curis incipis, et primo lapsus abire gradu: 'doomed man, at last there is one for whom you pine and grow wan; at last you have slipped and your downfall has begun'.

For *primus* attached adjectivally to a particular word but really going adverbially with the sentence or another part of the sentence cf. Virg. *Aen.* v, 857 *uix primos inopina quies laxauerat artus*; *Aen.* XI, 573–4 *ut primis uestigia plantis institerat*; *Aen.* X, 241–2 *surge age et aurora socios ueniente uocari primus in arma iube*, 426–8 *Lausus…primus Abantem interimit*. For *lapsus gradu* cf. Seneca, *Const. Sap.* XIX, 3 *iniurias uero ut uulnera...non deiectus ne motus quidem gradu sustineat.* For *abire* of downward motion cf. Ov. *Fast.* II, 73 *Titan abiturus in undas*; *Met.* XI, 791–2 *inque profundum pronus abit* (a diver); Lucan V, 135 *in immensas cineres abiere cauernas.*

[*primo...gradu* naturally suggests to us the English phrase 'take the first *step* down the slippery slope'. But *abire* suggests rather the combination *lapsus gradu* = 'losing your *foothold*'. Hence the interpretation set out above. But it is possible that both ideas are present.]

9. illarum: i.e. the *deceptae puellae* of line 5.

10. multarum miseras...uices: here *miseras uices* must mean either (1) *tristem ultionem*; or (2) *miserarum ultionem*. For the transfer of ephithet required by (2) cf. perhaps Stat. *Ach.* II, 43 *resides causas* = 'reason of my delay'.

12. nec noua quaerendo semper amicus eris: this seems to be intended as equivalent to a Greek compound beginning φιλο-. For the adjective *amicus* with the same value as φίλος has in such compounds cf. Cic. *N.D.* II, 43 (*Fortuna*) *amica uarietati*; Hor. *Epist.* I, ii, 26 *amica luto sus*; Silius Ital. XIII, 723 *auro Curium non umquam...amicum.* If the explanation suggested is right, the meaning will be: 'and no longer will you be always (*non semper*) on the hunt for new adventures (*amicus eris noua quaerendo*)'.

13. haec ego...doctus: sc. *dixi* or *sum*. Comparison with I, xvi, 45 suggests the former.

15. uidi ego te toto uinctum languescere collo: the picture is not altogether clear. *uinctum* evidently describes a close embrace, and is used in a related sense by Apuleius, *Apol.* XII (*Venerem*) *corpora complexu uincientem.* It looks therefore as though *uidi...uinctum languescere* here is parallel in meaning to *complexa morientem...puella uidimus* in I, x, 5–6. In the phrase *toto...collo* the adjective *toto* has certainly the value of an adverb and means 'wholly'. It may be that the man's neck is said to be involved 'wholly' in the embrace because not only are the girl's arms tightly around his neck but also his neck is pressed closely against hers. Or it may be that *toto ..collo* goes primarily with *languescere*.

· **17. et cupere optatis animam deponere uerbis**: 'and want to die for joy of (because of) her sweet words (*or the longed-for words you hear*)'. Cf. Nepos, *Hann.* I, 3 *odium* *paternum erga Romanos sic conseruauit ut prius animam quam id deposuerit*; Prop. II, iv, 21 *alter saepe uno* (because of) *mutat praecordia uerbo*; III, xxv, 9 *limina iam nostris ualeant lacrimantia uerbis*; I, x, 5 *cum te complexa morientem, Galle, puella uidimus, et longa ducere uerba mora*.

[Many prefer to read *labris* in place of *uerbis* in this line.]

optatis: unlike the English 'desired' *optatus* does not necessarily imply that there has been a conscious or specific desire for the thing in question, and sometimes it has to be rendered 'sweet', 'precious', 'welcome', etc. Cf. Virg. *Aen.* IV, 619 *nec regno aut optata luce fruatur*; Cicero (Junior) in *Fam.* XVI, xxi *gratos tibi optatosque esse qui de me rumores afferuntur non dubito* (and earlier he speaks of the arrival of a letter as *exoptatus*, not—as the context shows—because it had been eagerly awaited, but because an item of news in it gave him keen pleasure).

21–2. Tyro daughter of Salmoneus was in love with the river Enipeus, and Neptune (= Poseidon) being in love with Tyro disguised himself as the river. The scene of the story is variously set, in Thessaly or in Elis. Poseidon had a sanctuary at Taenarus, the southernmost cape of the Peloponnese.

21, 23. non sic...nec sic: the point of comparison is partly the response of the woman, partly the ardour of the lover.

22. facili: i.e. that meets response.

23–4. Oetaeis: Hercules ended his mortal life on Mount Oeta, where he burned himself on a pyre of his own building. He was immediately deified, and in his character as an Olympian god was husband of Hebe. Propertius here appears (with or without authority) to conceive him as united with Hebe, on Mount Oeta, immediately after his deification.

28. te tuus ardor aget: 'will give you no rest'; cf. I, xxii, 5 *cum Romana suos egit discordia ciuis* ('drove them to their doom').

29. proxima Ledae: cf. I, xx, 6 *proximus...Hylae*; Ov. *Met.* XII, 398 *pectoraque artificum laudatis proxima signis*.

30. Ledae partu: the three children cannot include the Dioscuri, as the comparison is with a woman. In Euripides, *Iph. Aul.* 49 three daughters of Leda are mentioned: Phoebe, Clytaemnestra and Helen.

31. illa sit...blandior: i.e. no heroine of Greece of old could match her charms.

Inachiis: Inachus was legendary founder of Argos. Here

Inachiis apparently stands for 'Argive (*or* Greek) of the legendary age'.

heroinis: Greek word-form, and Greek rhythm.

35. qui tibi sit felix, quoniam nouus incidit, error: 'and since this is a new experience of love that has befallen you, may it turn out happily'. [Here *qui* is a conjecture for *quae* of the MSS.]

36. et, quodcumque uoles, una sit ista tibi: 'and may she be all your heart's desire'; *or* 'and may she henceforth be your only love, whether you *will* (cf. line 6) or no'. [*quodcumque* is an emendation of the *quocumque* of the MSS.]

XIV

This elegy is complementary to Elegy vi, which like this one (and the first and last elegies of the whole book) is addressed to Tullus. There the lover is contrasted with the man of action: here the pleasures of riches are contrasted with those of love, to the advantage of the latter.

The detailed motive introduced here in lines 15–16 and 19–22 occurs also in Tibullus, I, ii, 77–8:

> quid Tyrio recubare toro sine amore secundo
> prodest, cum fletu nox uigilanda uenit?

1. Tiberina...unda: 'by the Tiber's side'; cf. Virg. *Aen.* VIII, 610 *ut* (*natum*) *egelido secretum flumine uidit* ('alone beside a cool stream').

2. Mentoreo: by Mentor, a silversmith of the fourth century B.C., celebrated for his chasing, engraving, etc.

5–6. et nemus omne satas intendat uertice siluas, urgetur quantis Caucasus arboribus: 'and though (in your grounds) those planted trees stand straight and tall, tall as the trees that tower on Caucasus'. For the relationship of *nemus* and *siluas* cf. Ov. *A.A.* III, 689 *silua nemus non alta facit;* the trees are *silua* and the group they compose is *nemus*—a copse, grove, orchard, etc. or in this case probably a 'plantation' in or in the precinct of a villa, for which there is no convenient word in English; cf. Tib. III, iii, 15 *nemora in domibus sacros imitantia lucos*, and Hor. *Epist.* I, x, 22 *inter uarias nutritur silua columnas*, and the orchard, attached to the palace of Alcinous, in *Odyssey* VII, 114 ἔνθα δὲ δένδρεα μακρὰ πεφύκασι τηλεθόωντα, etc. Such an orchard or plantation is a symbol of luxurious wealth; cf. III, ii, 13 *nec mea Phaeacas aequant pomaria siluas*, etc., and in the present passage lines 7–8. By *satas...siluas* are indicated artificially planted trees as opposed to those that grow spontaneously in nature.

The expression *nemus...intendat uertice siluas* is difficult. It seems to be a transitive form of what is put intransitively in Virg. *Georg.* II, 291–2 *aesculus...quae quantum uertice ad auras...tantum radice ad Tartara tendit.* There is no difficulty about the choice of *intendo*, which is used of stretching out the hands skyward or in other directions, and of straining the vision as far as it will reach. Nor is there difficulty about the use of singular *uertice* with reference to plural *siluas*. The trouble is simply the lack of an indirect object such as *caelo, ad auras* or the like to complete the meaning of the verb. As none the less the sentence is grammatical and the description intelligible and appropriate to its context, it is reasonable to accept this as another instance of Propertius' free use of language. The presence of the word *uertice* leaves no doubt anyway about the direction of *intendit.*

[Some take *intendat uertice* to mean 'stretches along the hill crest'. But this gives a strange meaning to *intendo* as applied to *siluas.* And *uertex* seems usually to mean specifically a peak and not a ridge. And there is nothing else in the context to suggest that a hill is part of the picture. Compare also the use of *uertice* with the simple verb *tendo* in the passage from Virgil quoted above.]

7. ista: the wealth and comforts enjoyed by the person (Tullus) whom Propertius is addressing.

9. quietem: by an extension of its meaning, = 'night', as in I, x, 1.

optatam: see on I, xiii, 17.

11. Pactoli: the Pactolus in Lydia was at one time a gold-bearing river.

14. dum me fata perire uolent: for the future simple indicative with *dum* = 'until' cf. Virg. *Georg.* IV, 412–13 *contende...uincla...donec talis erit mutato corpore qualem uideris*; Plaut. *Amph.* 470–3 *erroris ambo ego illos et dementiae complebo... adeo usque satietatem dum capiet pater illius quam amat.*

17. nulla mihi tristi praemia sint Venere: 'I want no riches if Venus frowns on me'. *tristi...Venere* seems to be an ablative absolute used to express a condition; but the idea of an ablative of price may also be present. *praemia* here means 'riches' or 'good things' as in *praemia uitae* in Lucr. III, 899; but it may also contain the idea 'compensation'.

19. Arabium...limen: according to *Pliny, N.H.* XXXVI, 59 the Romans of an earlier day believed that onyx was found in Arabia only, so onyx may be meant here.

22. uariis serica textilibus: 'silken tapestries'. The construction may be explained as on I, ii, 2, or *uariis...textilibus* may be a kind of instrumental ablative with *releuant*.

24. Alcinoi munera: 'the gifts of Alcinous', if we take *munera* in its normal meaning; cf. *Odyssey* VIII, 392, where Alcinous bestows rich gifts on Odysseus. But the reference is suggested by the thought of Alcinous' splendid orchard, which Gallus' plantation emulates; cf. 5–8 above and III, ii, 13. It may be, therefore, that *munera* here is used, by a trope, for 'luxuries', as at I, ii, 4.

XV

A lecture to Cynthia, like Elegy ii. Propertius apparently is ill (for no other meaning for *periclo* in line 3 will adequately fit the context). Cynthia is slow to come and visit him; and when she does appear she is made-up and dressed-up in a manner not at all appropriate to the concern she ought to feel about Propertius but designed evidently to catch the eye of other men. At line 25 there is an abrupt transition; it seems that Cynthia is about to defend herself against the first part of Propertius' complaint, when he interrupts her and starts again.

Sickness of the poet or of his mistress provides the situation also in Tib. I, iii and I, v, 9–20. The complaint of Cynthia's self-adornment here in lines 5–8 recalls the similar complaint in Elegy ii of the present book, and the terms (though not the application) of Tib. I, viii, 9–16. The complaint of false protestations in lines 25 ff. here is a topic that occurs also in Tib. I, ix, 1–2:

> quid mihi, si fueras miseros laesurus amores,
> foedera per diuos clam uiolanda dabas?

8. ut formosa nouo quae parat ire uiro: the adjective *formosa* here either (*a*) is used as a substantive, like for instance *pauper*; or (*b*) is predicative: 'like a woman who is preparing to go to a new lover looking beautiful', or as we should more likely say 'like a woman who beautifies herself to appear before a new lover'. The latter of these senses is doubtful, since strictly *formosus* should refer to natural beauty. For the former cf. II, xxviii, 13 *semper, formosae, non nostis parcere uerbis*.

10, 12. fleuerat...sederat: for the pluperfect, see on I, iii, 17.

13. dolebat: sc. *eum*, 'she was sorry for him'; cf. I, xvi, 24 *me dolet aura*. So too in line 17 *anxia* = 'anxious for his safety'. This is the point of *quamuis numquam post haec uisura* in line 13.

15-16. Alphesiboea..., etc.: this couplet is misplaced in the MSS., for *nec sic* in 17 must clearly follow the long sentence beginning *at non sic* in 9. The misplacement is intelligible because *laetitiae* in 14 has the same ending as *pudicitiae* in 18. The examples quoted seem to be disposed so as to rise to a climax: Calypso grieved, Hypsipyle never loved again, Evadne killed herself for her husband, Alphesiboea went even further and killed her brother.

15. Alphesiboea: her brothers killed her husband Alcmaeon because, being separated from her by exile, he had taken another wife. According to one version of the legend, which Propertius here follows, Alphesiboea avenged Alcmaeon by killing them.

18. Hypsipyle: queen of Lemnos who entertained Jason and fell in love with him, when the Argonauts put in at Lemnos on their outward voyage.

20. hospitio stands for *hospite*, as *coniugium* stands for *coniugem* at III, xiii, 20.

21. Euadne: wife of Capaneus, who was blasted with a thunderbolt by Jupiter (= Zeus) on account of an impious boast. Evadne threw herself upon his funeral pyre.

elata is specifically appropriate to a dead person's body being carried to pyre or grave in the regular way, and so not strictly appropriate to the end of Evadne; and this is the point of the phrase. We might translate: 'found her own funeral on her husband's pyre'.

22. fama: 'glory of...', the result standing for the cause. This particular usage is common to Latin and English.

25. desine iam...: the connexion of thought with what has preceded seems to be this: 'You have shown yourself (lines 1 ff.) insincere in your protestations of affection. Do not now renew these protestations, lest the gods this time take notice of your perjury.'

27–8. audax a nimium, nostro dolitura periclo, si quid forte tibi durius inciderit: Cynthia is blamed for risking heaven's displeasure, because Propertius will suffer through her suffering, if any grave misfortune befalls her.

29–30. nulla prius uasto labentur flumina ponto, annus et inuersas duxerit ante uices,...: for the content of the hexameter ('sooner will rivers cease to flow down to the sea...') cf. Virg. *Aen* I, 607 *in freta dum fluuii current*, etc. For the dative *ponto* after *labuntur* cf. Lucan vi, 362 *Ionio fluit inde mari*. For the combination of an inversion of the natural order of things in the pentameter with an adynaton of another kind in the hexameter cf. III, xix, 5–6 *flamma per incensas citius sedetur aristas, fluminaque ad fontis sint reditura caput.*

[*nulla prius* in 28 is a conjecture for *multa prius* of the MSS. Some would retain the MS. reading and punctuate *multa prius: uasto labentur flumina ponto* = 'before that, all manner of things will happen: rivers will flow back from (*ponto* being ablative) the sea, etc.' But a sentence intended to show that the natural order of things is reversed would surely make this more forcibly plain.]

32. sis quodcumque voles, non aliena tamen: two alternative renderings deserve consideration. (*a*) 'be what you will, only do not forsake me for another'. This is the most obviously natural meaning of the Latin, and though it does not *match* the meaning of the preceding hexameter it *fits* with it perfectly well. (*b*) 'you can be what you will, only you cannot cease to be my love'. This would match the meaning of the hexameter; and the sense of *aliena* required ('not cared for by...', 'a subject of indifference to...') is illustrated by Ov. *R.A.* 681 and *Trist.* IV, iii, 67. But it is very doubtful whether, out of the permissive-concessive *sis* of *sis quodcumque voles*, we can really supply *potes esse* to go with *non aliena*; the value of 'can' in the first member of the English rendering above is not identical with its value in the second member.

33. tam is an obviously necessary correction for *quam* of the MSS. The point of this line will appear from lines 34–6.

36. ut tibi suppositis exciderent manibus: before this we have to supply in thought a verb of praying to govern the *ut*, for Cynthia's oath by her eyes must have been in the form 'if I prove to have lied, then may these eyes of mine fall out into my hands'.

39. quis te cogebat: 'what need was there for you to?' The false pallor and forced tears were of her own contriving.

multos pallere colores: apparently an application to pallor of the colloquial Greek idiom seen in παντοδαπὰ ἤφιει χρώματα (Plato, *Lysis* 222B) which really refers to blushing. Pallor may have a variety of tinges.

40. ducere: draw out, i.e. 'force to flow'.

41. quis: neuter plural ablative. It refers either generally to the arts attributed to Cynthia in lines 35–40, or specifically to her eyes (line 40).

42. o nullis tutum credere . . .: i.e. *non est tutum ullis credere* . . .

XVI

A house-door is represented as speaking, complaining of the conduct of the lady who lives in the house and of the importunity of a lover who troubles the door with his pathetic appeals. A specimen of these appeals is given in lines 17–44.

This is Propertius' variant of a motive that is recurrent in ancient love poetry. In its simplest form the lover addresses the lady as he stands outside her closed door; examples of this are *A.P.* v, xxii (Callimachus) and Hor. *Od.* III, x. In Tib. I, ii, 7–14 and in lines 17–44 of Propertius' elegy here the lover addresses the door itself; in Ov. *Am.* I, vi he addresses the doorkeeper. In Cat. LXVII (not a love poem) we have a conversation between door and poet: in the present elegy the door speaks a monologue.

It is not clear that the woman referred to in this elegy is Cynthia. That the lover's complaint here and the woman's complaint in iii, 35–46 are the converse of one another has already been observed in the introductory note to Elegy iii.

2. ianua Tarpeiae nota pudicitiae: *pudicitiae* could be either dative, or genitive (cf. Hor. *Od.* II, ii, 6 *notus in fratres animi paterni*). The point of *Tarpeiae* is lost to us. The Tarpeia of the story told later by Propertius in IV, iv would not serve as a symbol of *pudicitia*, being a Vestal virgin who betrayed her country because of a passion she had conceived for the hostile commander. On the other hand the name has associations of dignity and antiquity through *mons Tarpeius* = the Capitoline hill, and a Tarpeia who according to Plutarch was one of the original Vestals appointed by King Numa.

3. inaurati...currus: i.e. triumphal chariots. Previous

occupants of the house had won triumphs and brought captives
to their home as slaves.

7. **non desunt. . .pendere:** cf. Tac. *Hist.* I, xxxvi *nec deerat
Otho. . .adorare uulgus, iacere oscula. . . .*

turpes: 'to my disgrace'.

8. **exclusi signa:** the discarded torches (discarded because
they have burned out in the waiting) are signs that an excluded
lover has been waiting outside the door. Cf. Pers. v, 165-6 *dum
Chrysidis udas ebrius ante fores exstincta cum face canto.* [*exclusi*
is a conjecture for *exclusis* of the MSS., which would mean that
the torches discarded outside the door are a sign to excluded
lovers that a more fortunate lover is within. But there is no
reason to suppose that it was usual to discard the torch, unless
it was burned out; and what causes it to burn out is the *waiting*.]

9-10. **nec possum infamis dominae defendere noctes,
nobilis obscenis tradita carminibus:** 'and I am helpless to
prevent the scandal of my mistress's nightly amours, as a result
of which I am myself disgraced and am made the subject of
ribald verses'. The door is lamenting its helplessness in a
humiliating situation. *defendere* (when it does not mean 'protect') can mean not only 'repulse' something bad that is im-
pending, but also 'stop' something bad that is already in course,
such as a fire, or a wrong already begun. *nobilis* can mean either
'famous' or 'notorious'; for the latter meaning cf. Cic. *Verr.* II,
iv, 73 *ille nobilis taurus* (of the brazen bull of Phalaris); either
meaning could stand·here, according as the word is construed
with the rest of the sentence; and the final meaning of the sentence will be much the same in either case.

11. **nec tamen illa suae,** etc.: there is an emphasis on *illa
suae.* The door cannot protect her reputation, and she won't
protect it herself.

12. **turpior et saecli uiuere luxuria:** *uiuere* is not attached
to *reuocatur* but to *turpior*, and *turpior* goes with *illa* in a kind of
apposition: 'in her way of living she is more dissolute even than
the age in which she lives'. There seems to be (cf. on I, x, 3) a
conflation·of two constructions: (*a*) *turpis uiuere luxuriose* (like
the construction *ridiculus totas simul absorbere placentas* in Hor.
Sat. II, viii, 24) and (*b*) *turpior saecli luxuria.*

13. **has inter:** sc. *noctes* from 9, which is rather far away but
not far enough to justify altering the text. For the construction
cf. Cic. *Fam.* XVI, x^i, 3 *nobis inter has turbas senatus tamen frequens*

flagitauit triumphum; Sall. *Jug.* LXVI, 3 *eos...inter epulas obtruncant.*

deflere: for this verb used intransitively cf. Plin. *Ep.* VIII, xvi, 5 *est enim quaedam etiam dolendi uoluptas, praesertim si in amici sinu defleas.*

14. a: 'as a result of...'; cf. Virg. *Georg.* I, 234 *torrida semper ab igni.* [It could alternatively be taken as an exclamation, in parenthesis.]

16. arguta: expressing both the raised voice and the fluency.

17. uel domina penitus crudelior ipsa: 'yet crueller, even, than your (*or* my) mistress herself'. *penitus* is intensive here; cf. Virg. *Ecl.* I, 66 *penitus toto diuisos orbe Britannos*; Velleius Pat. II, xxvii, 1 *uir...penitus Romano nomini infestissimus.*

20. reddere: 'deliver to your mistress'; cf. Cic. *Fam.* II, xvii, 1 *litteras a te mihi stator tuus reddidit Tarsi.*

22. in tepido limine: the threshold is called *tepidum* either because it is warmed by the body of the recumbent lover (as a chair is warm after someone has been sitting in it), or because after absorbing warmth from the sun, etc., during the day it cools off as the night proceeds until it is uncomfortably cool by the small hours of the morning. The former of these two possibilities is recommended by IV, vii, 20 *fecerunt tepidas pallia nostra uias.* Note that *tepidus* is used of things that are either warm or cool *by comparison with their normal or their previous state.*

23. sidera plena: see note on I, x, 8. [Many will prefer to accept the conjecture *prona.* The reference would then be to a time between midnight and dawn; cf. Virg. *Aen.* II, 8-9 *et iam nox umida caelo praecipitat, suadentque cadentia sidera somnos.* This gives a satisfying sequence: midnight, small hours, dawn. And an excellent sound-pattern.]

24. me dolet: 'is sorry for me'; cf. I, xv, 13 and note.

25. numquam negatives both *miserata* and *respondes.*

26. respondes...mutua: 'respond or make reply' (to my complaint). For the almost superfluous use of *mutua* cf. Ov. *Met.* I, 655 *nec mutua nostris dicta refers.*

28. uertat: 'direct its way towards'. The expression is a little odd and no clear parallel has been adduced. Cf. however for the intransitive use of *uerto* Tac. *Ann.* I, xviii, 3 *depulsi aemulatione...alio uertunt*, and the like.

29. saxo...Sicano: some say that what is meant is lava,

conceived as typically Sicilian because of Etna, etc.; others say
agate, of which Pliny (*N.H.* XXXVII, 139) affirms that it was in
Sicily that it was first discovered.

32. surget et inuitis spiritus in lacrimis: 'and in spite
of her, the tears and sighs will come'. For *surget* cf. the
English 'heave' a sigh.

34. nocturno...cadunt Zephyro: 'fall disregarded with
none but the wind and the night to heed them'; cf. I, xvii, 4
ingrato litore...cadunt 'fall disregarded on the unkind shore'.

38. quae solet ingrato dicere pota loco: this clause is a
substantive in apposition to *petulantia* in the preceding line:
'the kind of things that I say (my tongue says) when I'm drunk
and angry with my surroundings'. For a similar apposition
cf. I, xviii, 24 below.

[*ingrato* is a likely enough conjecture for *irato* of the MSS.;
cf. I, vi, 10 where the same conjecture is pretty certain. *pota*
is a far from certain conjecture for *tota* of the MSS. For the
construction of *pota* cf. Ov. *Fast.* v, 335 *tempora cinguntur pota
coronis*; and for the point cf. Tib. II, v, 101 *ingeret hic potus...
maledicta puellae.*]

**39–40. ut me tam longa raucum patiare querela sollicitas
triuio peruigilare moras**: 'that you should leave me like this
to grow hoarse from much complaining and to pass long nights
in sleepless torment at the street corner'.

42. osculaque impressis nixa dedi gradibus: probably one
should understand *tibi* from the preceding line: the lover kneels
on the steps and leans forward to press his kisses upon the door.

43. uerti me: in prayer; cf. Lucr. v, 1199 *uertier ad lapidem*;
Plin. *N.H.* XXVIII, 25 *in adorando dextram ad osculum referimus
totumque corpus circumagimus.*

44. debita...uota: the offerings are owed (*debita*) because
they have been vowed (*uota*).

occultis: i.e. furtively, because he would feel embarrassed
to be seen so behaving publicly in daytime, or because he does
not want to excite the suspicion of his rival.

47. semper: probably with *fletibus* = 'continual lamentations'; cf. I, xxii, 2 *pro nostra semper amicitia*; also I, iii, 44.

47–8. 'And so because of my mistress's misdeeds and her
lover's endless lamentations I am slandered in unkind gossip all
the time.' For *differor* cf. I, iv, 22.

XVII

This and the following Elegy xviii are soliloquies supposed to be uttered by the poet in unusual surroundings. Here he is in a storm at sea, having of his own accord torn himself away from Cynthia. In xviii he is in a lonely place amid wild scenery, lamenting the cruelty of Cynthia, who has banished him from her favour.

Propertius imagines the storm here to be due to Cynthia's curses on him for his departure. A curse on a departing person (*not* however a lover, by any means) is represented in Hor. *Epod.* x, where the poet prays for and imagines a storm that is to overtake someone who has incurred his displeasure.

The attentions which Propertius imagines Cynthia would have paid him after death if he had remained with her (lines 19–24) are parallel with those imagined by Tibullus too (1, i, 59–64):

> te spectem, suprema mihi cum uenerit hora,
> et teneam moriens deficiente manu.
> flebis et arsuro positum me, Delia, lecto,
> tristibus et lacrimis oscula mixta dabis.
> flebis; non tua sunt duro praecordia ferro
> uincta, nec in tenero stat tibi corde silex.

2. **alcyonas**: birds symbolizing the sea—not necessarily in a calm state, as appears both from this poem and from III, vii, 61.

3. **Cassiope**: a harbour-town in Corcyra: cf. Cic. *Fam.* xvi, ix, 1 *in portum Corcyraeorum ad Cassiopen stadia CXX processimus.*

saluo: this is a plausible but not certain conjecture for *solito* of the MSS., which is certainly wrong and may be due to *-o lito-* in *ingrato litore* in the line below.

5. **quin etiam...prosunt tibi...uenti**: cf. also line 9 below. He imagines that Cynthia's imprecations on him for leaving her are the cause of the storm.

6. **increpat aura minas**: cf. Virg. *Aen.* IX, 503–4 *at tuba terribilem sonitum...increpuit.*

7. **nullane placatae ueniet fortuna procellae?**: 'Can there be no change? Will the storm never abate?' The genitive *procellae* is a genitive of definition, as in Virg. *Aen.* I, 27 *spretae-*

que iniuria formae. With *fortuna* here meaning a favourable change of circumstances cf. Virg. *Aen.* IX, 41 *si qua interea fortuna fuisset*, where it means an unfavourable change of circumstances; and Georg. III, 452 *praesens fortuna laborum* (remedy).

11–12. an poteris siccis mea fata reponere ocellis, ossaque nulla tuo nostra tenere sinu?: 'to lay me to my rest, without a tear, and hold no mortal remnants of me in your lap —will you be hard enough for that?'. The poet assumes that Cynthia will preside over his exequies, despite the quarrel, as he does also at line 21 below, and in II, xiii, 16 ff. Since his body will have been lost at sea, she will not be able to gather his ashes after cremation, in the way proper to the nearest mourner: cf. IV, i. 127–8 *ossaque legisti...patris*; Lucan IX, 58 *tepida uestes implere fauilla*. But she will have to go through a form used when the body was not available, erecting a cenotaph and offering sacrifices at it; as is done for Deiophobus at Virg. *Aen.* VI, 555, and anticipated by Nisus at *Aen.* IX, 215. The obscure phrase *mea fata reponere* must refer to this; and the wording of it is explained by II, xiii, 22 *in Attalico mors mea* (= my corpse) *nixa toro*; iv, viii, 25 *dabit uenalia fata* (= let himself be killed, for hire); Avienus, *Aratea* 211 *portitor...Charon Thesidae fata* (= the shade of the dead Hippolytus) *uehebat*; and then further Virg. *Aen.* VI, 655 *tellure repostos*; Sil. It. XIII, 404 *mactare repostis...umbris...nigras pecudes*. In Hor. *Od.* I, x, 17 *reponis* is said of bringing souls to their resting-place below. [I earlier printed *reposcere*, taking it as 'ask how I met my end'. But in Tac. *Hist.* III, 12 *quid dicturos reposcentibus aut prospera aut aduersa* it seems to mean 'demand a justification of...' rather than 'ask the story of...'.]

15. nonne fuit leuius dominae peruincere mores: here *mores* evidently = 'humours', a sense illustrated also by the adjective *morosus*, by the phrase *morem gerere* and by Plaut. *Most.* 286 *amator meretricis mores sibi emit auro et purpura*; 'humours' may be good, bad or simply capricious, according to context. *peruincere* can mean simply 'master' or 'get the better of', or (with an *ut* clause or the like) 'prevail on to...'. So the meaning of the line before us must be: 'would it not have been easier to contend with my mistress's humours until I won my way?' It says rather more than Virg. *Ecl.* II, 14–15 *nonne fuit satius tristes Amaryllidis iras atque superba pati fastidia?*

18. **Tyndaridas.** Castor and Pollux, invoked as saviours by sailors in distress.

quaerere here, as quite commonly, has the special meaning 'look for and fail to find'. *optatos* no doubt here means 'prayed for', since this is one of the regular meanings of *optare*, cf. *optare aliquid uotis..., a dis immortalibus optare ut...,* etc. The meaning of the sentence thus is: 'pray in vain for Castor and Pollux to come to our aid'.

19–20. **illic si qua meum sepelissent fata dolorem, ultimus et posito staret amore lapis:** '[if I had died at Rome] if there death had laid my sorrow in the grave, and there a stone now stood to mark my love's last rest'.

22. **molliter et tenera poneret ossa rosa:** (?) 'and would have laid my bones to rest with offering of roses'. As far as we know, the flowers were laid *on* the tomb or urn; cf. IV. vii, 33 *nulla mercede hyacinthos inicere*; Juv. VII, 208 *in* ('on') *urna perpetuum uer.* [But both the imperfect subjunctive and the ablative in this construction are strange. One wonders whether perhaps Propertius has construed *poneret* as if it were *sterneret* and r ...s 'strew my grave with roses'; cf. Tib. I, vii, 50 *multo tempora funde mero*; Virg. *Aen.* XII, 174 *pateris altaria libant*; Juv. VII, 47 *posita est orchestra cathedris.* This would give value to the imperfect, referring to a process, and one repeated on anniversaries.]

molliter: cf. the prayer in Ov. *Trist.* III, iii, 76 *Nasonis molliter ossa cubent* (rest in peace). It suggests the woman's tenderness too.

23. **extremo puluere:** 'over my ashes, at the end'.

24. **ut...foret:** a verb of praying has to be supplied in thought to govern the *ut* clause.

26. **soluite uela:** the Nereids do not actually spread the sails, but their action results in this; cf. II, xxvi, 49 *iam deus amplexu uotum persoluit*, where the vow is evidently the girl's vow and not the god's, but the god's action results in its being paid.

27. **labens:** *labor* is sometimes used of a ship gliding through the water, cf. I, xx, 19–20 *labentem...ratem.* But as love is winged it is more natural to think of him here as gliding down from the sky.

28. **mansuetis socio parcite litoribus:** 'have mercy on a fellow-sufferer, and may your shores be kind to him'.

XVIII

See the introductory note to the preceding elegy, to which this is a counterpart. Here the setting, amid wild scenery, recalls that of Corydon's lament in Virg. *Ecl.* II, 3–5:

> tantum inter densas, umbrosa cacumina, fagos
> assidue ueniebat. ibi haec incondita solus
> montibus et siluis studio iactabat inani...,

and of Gallus' despair in *Ecl.* X, 13–15:

> illum etiam lauri, etiam fleuere myricae,
> pinifer illum etiam sola sub rupe iacentem
> Maenalus et gelidi fleuerunt saxa Lycaei...,

and 52–4:

> certum est in siluis, inter spelaea ferarum
> malle pati, tenerisque meos incidere amores
> arboribus....

It will be remembered (see on Elegy viiiA) that Eclogue X is said to contain echoes of Gallus' own poems.

4. si modo: either 'if perchance...', meaning 'in the hope that...'; or (with a strong stop after *dolores* in the preceding line) 'oh that...may...'. For *si* introducing a wish cf. Virg. *Aen.* VI, 187–8 *si nunc se nobis ille aureus arbore ramus ostendat nemore in tanto!*, and (probably) 882 *si qua fata aspera rumpas!*; also English 'if only...!' and Greek εἰ γάρ.

8. cogor habere notam: 'am branded as disgraced'.

9. crimina: the best MSS. have *carmina* = 'spells', but *crimina*, conjectured long ago, makes better sense (between the last and next sentences) and is likely to be right.

11–12. sic...pedes: 'as surely as I wish you may return to me, traitress, no other fair one's foot has passed my door'. *sic* thus construed with a wish or prayer in the subjunctive is regularly used to reinforce assertions in the indicative.

nostro limine: 'through my door'.

13. quamuis multa tibi dolor hic meus aspera debet: the 'cruel hurts' may be either those suffered by Propertius and owed to Cynthia as their origin, or hurts owed to Cynthia as vengeance for what she has done. Both ideas may well be present.

15. ut tibi sim merito semper furor: 'that you should have just cause to be [? thus] always angry with me'. The point is in *merito*.

17. an quia...: this is the second possible explanation of his banishment, considered only to be rejected; the first came at line 10; a third will come at line 23.

parua: 'too little'; see note on I, v, 25.

19. si quos habet arbor amores: either 'trees that are acquainted with love' (for each tree has its nymph with which it can be identified); or 'that have tokens of love carved on them' (cf. Virg. *Ecl.* x, 54 *crescent illae, crescetis, amores*).

20. Arcadio pinus amica deo: a reference to a myth about the love of Pan for Pitys (the pine-tree, or its nymph). No similar story is known about the *fagus* mentioned just before.

21. teneras...sub umbras: the shade of the foliage is 'delicate', but also 'amorous' and so sympathetic, for these trees have been in love; the adjective *teneras* has thus a double meaning here.

23-6. an tua...queri: 'or is it that your cruelty has moved me to bitter complaints—complaints known only to the door that tells no tales? No—it has been my way always to bear your proud arrogance humbly, and never cry aloud at your misdeeds.'

23. an tua quod peperit nobis iniuria curas: the terms in which the suggestion is repudiated in lines 25-6 show that *curas* here means resentment on Propertius' part expressed in complaints; this seems to be the meaning of *curae* in Virg. *Aen.* XII, 801-2 *ne te tantus edit tacitam dolor et mihi curae saepe tuo dulci tristes ex ore recursent*. For *iniuria* = 'cruelty' or 'unreasonableness' cf. Ter. *Heaut.* 991-3 *matres omnes filiis... auxilio paterna in iniuria solent esse*. For the thought cf. Prop. II, xviii, 1 ff. *assiduae multis odium peperere querelae; ...si quid doluit forte, dolere nega*.

24. quae solum tacitis cognita sunt foribus: in apposition to *curas* or to the general sense of the hexameter; cf. I, xvi, 38.

27. diuini fontes: cf. Theocritus, VIII, 33 ἄγκεα καὶ ποταμοὶ θεῖον γένος; Apollonius Rhod. I, 1208 κρήνης ἱερὸν ῥόον; Virg. *Ecl.* I, 52 *fontis sacros*. The conventional epithet seems a little odd beside *frigida* and *dura*. One would expect here an epithet corresponding in tone to *frigida* and *inculto*.

XIX

A poem of feeling. Propertius' thoughts are turned towards death, and he prays that Cynthia may remain faithful to him when he is gone, as he surely will remain faithful to her, even in the world below. He concludes with the wish that they should enjoy their love to the full while they can still do so here in life. The opening and concluding sentiments have a certain affinity with those of Tib. i, i, 59 ff.; compare the lines of the Tibullan elegy quoted above (on Elegy xvii) and also lines 69–70:

> interea dum fata sinunt iungamus amores:
> iam ueniet tenebris mors adoperta caput.

Propertius' imagining of the underworld here in lines 11–14 has its counterpart in the imagining of the underworld by Tibullus in Tib. i, iii, 57–82, though the resulting scenes are wholly dissimilar.

This elegy, of a power equalled only by Elegy i, is the last elegy on the Cynthia theme in the present book.

2. nec moror: 'I do not mind about...'.

5. puer: Love.

6. ut meus oblito puluis amore uacet: 'that I could forget my love, when I am dust, and be at peace'. For *uacare* used absolutely (though in a slightly different sense) cf. i, xiii, 2 *quod abrepto solus amore uacem.* For *oblitus* used passively cf. Virg. *Ecl.* ix, 53 *nunc oblita mihi tot carmina.*

uacet: a potential subjunctive, giving the sense 'could', as well as a consecutive subjunctive governed by *ut*.

7. Phylacides: Protesilaus, a Thessalian (cf. 10), grandson of Phylacus, was the first Greek to be killed at Troy. His ghost was allowed to visit his widow, Laodamia, and when the visit was ended she killed herself.

illic: 'in the world below'. A jump in thought; cf. on i, i, 31, i, xi, 8, i, xvii, 26, etc.

11. quidquid ero: 'whatever shall be my state'; cf. i, xi, 26.

13–18. 'Never mind, though all the fabled beauties there should come in a throng to greet me, all those whom the Achaeans won as spoil from Troy—for the beauty of none of them can please me more than yours. And never mind how long a span of life awaits you (may just Earth allow that it be long indeed) before you can follow me—for your ghost when it comes at last will find me loving you and pining for you none the less.'

For the singular *chorus* in line 13 in apposition to the plural *heroinae* cf. Stat. *Theb.* IV, 651 *mox turba ruunt*, etc. For *hoc ita* in line 16 cf. Virg. *Aen.* X, 623 *meque hoc ita ponere sentis*. In the same line *Tellus* is *iusta* because thought of as not claiming Cynthia sooner than is kind or right. For *ossa* in line 18 meaning 'ghost' or 'shade' cf. IV, v, 4 (Cerberus) *ieiuno terreat ossa sono*, and IV, xi, 20 (Aeacus) *in mea...uindicet ossa*, etc.

The subjunctives *ueniant* in line 13 and *remorentur* in line 17 are (I think) of the same kind as *oderint* in *oderint dum metuant*, which expects no apodosis but contains a meaning complete in itself: 'let them hate me (if they will)' = 'never mind if they hate me'; cf. Lucan I, 311 *ueniat longa dux pace solutus...etc.*

If this view of the main construction is correct, I think that *quarum* in line 15 is most easily taken as = *nam earum*; and that *cara tamen lacrimis ossa futura meis* in line 18 probably stands in apposition to *te* in the preceding line; or it may be vocative. In line 17 *quamuis* will have its primary sense ('ever so...', 'as ...as can be') and go closly with the adjective *longae*.

There can be no certainty about the above analysis of this confused and breathless passage, and the reader may well prefer to construe it otherwise. The general tenor of it is of course clear enough.

19. quae: 'and may you still living have the same feeling for me when I am ashes'—i.e. the same love that he has promised *he* will still feel for *her* when he is dead. (*quae* is neut. plur.)

mea...fauilla: a very free use of the ablative, meaning either 'at my ashes', i.e. at his tomb (where the ashes would be preserved in an urn); or 'on account of my ashes', i.e. on account of him when he is dead (cf. the use of the ablative in *uno mutat praecordia uerbo* at II, iv, 21).

20. tum mihi non ullo mors sit amara loco: either 'then death (i.e. the coming of death) will have no bitterness for me, wherever it comes to me'; or 'then death (i.e. the state of death) will have no bitterness for me, wherever my abode (i.e. even in some grim place in the underworld)'.

22. abstrahat, heu, nostro puluere iniquus amor: see on I, vii, 16. For the plain ablative after *abstraho* cf. Ov. *Met.* XIII, 658 *abstrahit inuitas gremio genitoris*.

24. certa puella: the context shows that this must mean

'*even* a woman whose heart is true'.

minis: literally 'threats' (of what the lover will do to her or to himself if he is refused). But the word here may have a slightly extended meaning, such as 'protestations'; cf. on I, x, 26.

XX

This is an essay in a Hellenistic genre, the brief elegiac narrative of an episode from mythology. Its immediate model is Theocritus XIII, in which also, as here, the rape of Hylas is recounted and introduced by a brief address to a friend. The rape of Hylas is also recounted by Apollonius Rhodius, *Argonautica* I, 1182 ff. On the difference between Propertius and his Theocritean model I quote a friend: 'Theocritus' poem has a very tenuous connexion with real life, whereas Propertius' springs from an actual situation: Gallus and his Hylas and the danger that some pretty girl will separate the two. Propertius amusingly equates Roman girls with *Nymphae* and *Ausoniae Adryades* (lines 11–12). He refers to *Aniena...unda* and *Gigantea...ora* because Baiae (in the latter area) is a fashionable holiday resort and therefore dangerous (cf. Elegy xi) and the neighbourhood of Tibur (on the Anio) has fashionable villas and so is dangerous too. All things considered, I find I, xx a much more entertaining and pointed poem than Theocritus XIII.'

2. uacuo...ex animo: 'see that you heed my warning and do not forget it'. Cf. Sall. *Jug.* LII *Rutilium...animo* (ablative of respect) *uacuum* = 'unsuspecting'.

3. fortuna: here = 'disaster', i.e. bad fortune; cf. on I, xvii, 7. For *occurrere* of something adverse or unfavourable cf. Ov. *Am.* III, xii, 3 *quodue putem sidus nostris occurrere fatis...?*

4. Minyis: the Minyae are the Argonauts, so called from the Thessalian king Minyas from whom most of them were descended.

Ascanius: a river in Bithynia near which the adventure that is to be related took place.

6. Theiodamanteo proximus ardor Hylae: Theiodamas was Hylas' father. *ardor* = 'love', meaning object of love.

proximus...Hylae: 'almost as fair as Hylas'; cf. I, xiii, 29 *proxima Ledae.*

7. huic: a conjecture for *hunc* of the MSS., to fit the syntax of *cupidas defende rapinas* in line 11.

leges: one meaning of *lego* is 'to pick or wind one's way', e.g. among obstacles or along a coastline. Here it is used of walking along a river bank.

umbrosae flumina siluae: perhaps the Clitumnus, for cf. II, xix, 25–6 *qua formosa suo Clitumnus flumina luco integit*....

9. Gigantea...litoris ora: apparently the Phlegraean fields in the coastal region near Cumae, for Strabo (V, iv, 6) associates this with the legendary battle between the gods and the giants.

10. siue ubicumque uago fluminis hospitio: 'or dallying anywhere beside a winding stream'.

12. Adryasin: this is a correction for *adriacis* of the MSS. A word meaning 'nymphs' is required. Ἀδρυάδες occurs in *A.P.* IX, dclxiv (an epigram of Paulus Silentiarius). Strictly Naiads rather than Dryads are here in question, but there is nothing odd about the use of the special name for nymphs in general; the names of Muses are used in the same way.

non minor: the nymphs in Italy are no less amorous than those who stole Hylas from Hercules.

13. ne tibi sint: 'lest your lot be...'; cf. I, xviii, 27–8 *pro quo diuini fontes et frigida rupes et datur inculto tramite dura quies.* The next couplet 15–16 explains the point. Gallus is to avoid the fate of Hercules, who lost Hylas and thereafter wandered fruitlessly over hill and dale in search of him.

14. neque expertos semper adire lacus: 'and go from spring to spring in endless quest' (literally 'and always be visiting springs you have not tried before'). This phrase is in effect a nominative, parallel to *montes* and *saxa* in the preceding line. For the passive sense of *expertos* in *neque expertos* cf. I, iii, 18 *expertae metuens iurgia saeuitiae*.

15–16. error...Herculis: cf. II, xx, 31 *atque inter Tityi uolucris mea poena uagetur*; and Greek phrases such as βίη Ἡρακληείη.

ignotis...in oris: 'in a strange land'.

16. indomito: 'cruel', 'unrelenting'. Cf. Cat. CIII, 2 *deinde esto quamuis saeuus et indomitus*; and *crudelis* in line 4 above.

Ascanio: this may be ablative of place ('by') or dative or both. Cf. on I, i, 14.

17. Pagasae: *Pagasa* (fem. sing.) or *Pagasae* (fem. plural); the Thessalian sea-town where the Argo was built, and from which its voyage began.

Argon: for this form of the accusative cf. Ov. *Tr.* II, 439 *Phasiacas Argon qui duxit in undas.* (In Ov. *Her.* VI, 65 and XII, 9 the manuscripts vary between *Argon* and *Argo.*)

17–20. Argon...applicuisse ratem: for the oddity of the ship Argo being said *applicuisse ratem* cf. I, xi, 11–12 *teneat clausam...Teuthrantis in unda...lympha*; Stat. *Theb.* II, 636–8 *lancea...cognata...pectora...telo conserit.*

19. Athamantidos undis: the Hellespont, Helle being daughter of Athamas.

20. Mysorum: Mysia includes the south shore of the Propontis.

22. mollia composita litora fronde tegit: they 'heap up leaves on the beach to make it soft lying for themselves'. *mollia* is proleptic.

23. ultra: 'further afield'.

23–4. processerat...quaerere: poetic infinitive of purpose or result after a verb of motion; cf. on I, i, 12.

24. raram sepositi quaerere fontis aquam: this may mean that spring-water was scarce in the region (cf. *rarus inuentu calculus*, etc.). But if so, the observation has not much point. It is for consideration whether *raram* is not here used for *non communem* = 'unsullied', or *tenuem* (cf. Ov. *Fast.* II, 250) = 'clear'. An out-of-the-way (*sepositus*) spring is less likely than a more accessible one to have been defiled or muddied by public use. Cf. *rarus* in the senses 'peerless' and 'select'.

25. Aquilonia proles: i.e. the sons of Boreas.

27. suspensis...palmis: as they hover, their hands are held ready to pounce.

28. oscula...ferre: 'give kisses'. Cf. II, vi, 8 *oscula nec desunt qui tibi iure ferant*; II, xviii, 18 *et canae totiens oscula ferre comae*; Ov. *A.A.* III, 310 *oscula ferre umero...libet.* The distinction between *oscula ferre* and *oscula carpere* (line 27, 'steal kisses') is no doubt chiefly verbal. But kisses can be stolen only from the mouth of the other person, whereas they can be given in other places as well.

supina: this must mean either that the winged assailant turns over on his back (like a shark biting) to administer the kiss, or that the kiss is given as he begins to move upward after a dive. Cf. Liv. XXX, x, 13 *uana pleraque utpote supino iactu tela in locum superiorem mittebant*; Ov. *Med. Fac.* 40 *nec redit in fontes unda supina suos.*

29–30. ille sub extrema pendens secluditur ala, et uolucres ramo summouet insidias: 'the boy bends forward and shelters his face as well as he can under his arm, and tries to beat off the winged attackers with a bough'. For *pendens* = 'leaning forward' cf. IV, viii, 21 *primo temone pependit* (of Cynthia leaning forward as she drives); Virg. *Ecl.* I, 75–6 *non ego uos posthac...dumosa pendere procul de rupe uidebo* (of goats appearing to lean forward over a precipice); Virg. *Aen.* X, 586 *pronus pendens in uerbera* (of a charioteer); also modern Italian *torre pendente* for the 'leaning tower' of Pisa. The idea in *sub extrema...secluditur ala* seems to be that the boy ducks his head as far down as he can[1] (cf. Ov. *Her.* IV, 70 *in extremis ossibus haesit amor* = 'deep in...') toward his armpit, while he also raises his arm somewhat—the face is then sheltered in the triangle formed by the flank, shoulder and upper arm. *ala* means rather more than the English 'armpit', for in Juv. XIV, 195 the *alae* of a recruit are prized by the recruiting officer for being *grandes*, and in Liv. IX, xli, 18–19 *umbonibus incussaque ala sternuntur hostes*.

31. cessit: 'are (is) gone'. The perfect has here the value of a historic present. [*cessit* is a conjecture to replace the corrupt *cesset* of the MS. tradition.]

Pandioniae...genus Orithyiae: Orithyia daughter of Erechtheus son of Pandion was mother of Zetes and Calais by Boreas.

32. Hamadryasin: a correction for the unintelligible *amadryas hinc* of the MSS. Here the word is used as a name for nymphs in general, though strictly Hamadryads are tree nymphs. Cf. line 13 above.

33. Arganthi: Arganthus here is the name used for what Apollonius Rhod. I, 1178 calls Ἀργανθώνειον ὄρος.

Pege: a correction for *phege* of the MSS. Cf. Apollonius Rhod. I, 1222, where Pegae (plural) is the name of the spring in which Hylas is lost. The verb *erat* here is singular, and it may be that Propertius made the name singular for convenience.

---

[1] His behaviour is exactly what we should expect. The interpretation given above, or one very like it, was advanced a century ago by the Revd. A H. Wratislaw. If *ala* in a sense other than 'wing' comes surprisingly to us in a context that includes winged creatures, we have to remember that *ala* in *both* senses was fully normal and familiar to a Roman: in our minds the sense 'wing' is disproportionately predominant because our experience of the Latin language is almost wholly literary.

35. nullae: comparable forms of the feminine dative occur several times in Terence (*Heaut.* 271, *Phorm.* 928, *Eun.* 1004) but are extremely rare in later authors. Tib. III, xii, 9=IV, vi, 9 (*ullae*) is another example.

41. nescius: perhaps 'absorbed', but probably rather 'wondering'; cf. Virg. *Aen.* VII, 381 *stupet inscia supra impubesque manus mirata uolubile buxum*, II, 307-8 *stupet inscius alto accipiens sonitum saxi de uertice pastor.*

42. errorem blandis tardat imaginibus: 'he dallied still lingering, fascinated by the reflections in the water'. (*errorem tardat* means 'delayed his dawdling steps'.)

43. palmis: standing here for 'hands', as in 27 above, and often.

45. Dryades: cf. on 13 and 32 above.

48. sonitum...fecit Hylas: *sonitum* must at least include a cry for help, since Hercules answers it in line 49. It may include the splash also. *sonitus* is not regularly used of the human voice; but cf. Virg. *Georg.* IV, 333-4 *at mater sonitum thalamo sub fluminis alti sensit*, where what she hears is Aristaeus' lament. [As there is no strictly proper Latin word for 'scream' one must be prepared for the adoption of a related word whose strict meaning is different, by the trope called κατάχρησις or *abusio*, for which see Quintilian VIII, vi, 34. A well-known instance is Virg. *Aen.* VI, 204 *auri per ramos aura refulsit.*]

49. sed: the thought, not fully expressed, is: 'but it was only a faint cry that the breeze bore back to him, his own name, coming from the depths of the pool'.

50. nomen ab extremis fontibus aura refert: here *ab extremis fontibus* = 'from the depths of the spring'; for this meaning of *extremus* cf. Ov. *Her.* IV, 70 *acer in extremis ossibus haesit amor.* The phrase *nomen...aura refert* must mean accordingly that the breeze carries to Hercules his own name (Hercules) called by Hylas in answer to him; and cf. Theocritus XIII, 58-9 τρὶς μὲν Ὕλαν ἄυσεν...τρὶς δ' ἄρ' ὁ παῖς ὑπάκουσεν· ἀραιὰ δ' ἵκετο φωνὰ ἐξ ὕδατος.... [However, *nomen...refert* could also mean 'carried back to him an echo of the name (Hylas) that he had called', and in Valerius Flaccus' account of the myth (III, 597) what answers Hercules is in fact an echo. It is quite possible that this overtone is present in Propertius' mind. Some editors change *fontibus* to *montibus* in spite of Theocritus XIII, 58-9.]

52. uisus: 'for it has seemed to me that you...'. Or possibly 'for I have seen you...'. For the possibility of *uideor* = 'I am seen to' cf. Lucr. v, 1198–9 *nec pietas ullast...uideri uertier ad lapidem;* also IV, 306–7.

XXI

A kinsman of Propertius lost his life (cf. I, xxii, 3–8) in connexion with the siege of Perusia in 41 B.C. His body was never buried (I, xxii, 8) and so cannot have been found. In this poem Propertius imagines his kinsman, wounded and dying, appealing to a passing fugitive, one of his fellow-soldiers, to take a message to his (the speaker's) sister, presumably his surviving next of kin. The form of the poem is based on a familiar type of grave-epigram, in which the dead man (in the present poem he is not dead but dying) addresses a passer-by—ξένος, παροδίτης, ναυτίλος or the like. The MS. tradition in line 6 makes the speaker ask the passer-by to conceal the circumstances of his death, but it is hard to conceive such a request being imagined by Propertius and made the subject of a poem, and impossible to reconcile such a request with the concluding request in line 10. It can safely be assumed, from what we know of ancient sentiment, that the speaker is asking for his sister to be informed of his fate; and further (given his situation) that he wishes his bones to be buried; cf. *A.P.* VII, dxxi (Callimachus):

> Κύζικον ἢν ἔλθῃς, ὀλίγος πόνος Ἱππακον εὑρεῖν
> καὶ Διδύμην· ἀφανὴς οὔτι γὰρ ἡ γενεή.
> καί σφιν ἀνιηρὸν μὲν ἐρεῖς ἔπος, ἔμπα δὲ λέξαι
> τοῦθ', ὅτι τὸν κείνων ὧδ' ἐπέχω Κριτίην.

and Horace, *Od.* I, xxviii, 21 ff.:

> me quoque deuexi rapidus comes Orionis
>   Illyricis notus obruit undis.
> at tu, nauta, uagae ne parce malignus harenae
>   ossibus et capiti inhumato
> particulam dare: sic, quodcumque minabitur Eurus
>   fluctibus Hesperiis, Venusinae
> plectantur siluae te sospite, multaque merces
>   unde potest tibi defluat...

(where, incidentally, the construction illustrates that of lines 5–6 in the present poem). The piece is of course to be understood as

a fiction, not as the record of a speech really made. The following
is a translation of the printed text. 'You, soldier, hastening to
escape a fate like mine (*or*, from the defeat which I shared),
wounded fugitive from the siegeworks around Perusia (*or*, from
the ramparts of Perusia), why at my groan do you turn your
staring eyes? I am one who was your fellow-soldier a little while
ago (*or*, in the recent battles). May you get safe home and make
your parents glad; and then remember this prayer of mine, and,
weeping, let my sister Acca know my fate: that I, Gallus,
escaped unhurt through Caesar's army, only to be murdered by
hands unknown. She will find many another dead man's bones
on the Etruscan hills. See that she knows that these are mine.'

   2. aggeribus: either the works thrown up around Perusia
by both sides during the siege (cf. Appian, *B.C.* v, 33), or simply
(by an extension of meaning) the ramparts of the city itself (cf.
Virg. *Aen.* XI, 382 *agger murorum*, etc.).

   3. turgentia lumina: starting out of his head, from ex-
haustion, or alarm, or both.

   torques: he turns his eyes suddenly at the sound. For *torqueo*
in this sense cf. Virg. *Aen.* III, 669 *uestigia torsit*, IV, 220 *oculos-
que ad moenia torsit*. (In *Aen.* VII, 448-9 *flammea torquens lumina*
refers to something different, an angry glare.)

   quid...?: the interrogative form is a literary 'figure', of
course. It means 'you need not be afraid'.

   4. proxima: there seems no reason why he should stress the
closeness of their association, and no reason to suppose that any
special relation existed between the two men, as their present
encounter is obviously fortuitous. It follows that *proxima* here
has a temporal meaning, like the adverb *proxime* in Caes. *B.G.*
III, 29 (*ciuitates*) *quae proxime bellum fecerant*. For the adjective
used adverbially cf. the treatment of *primus* in poetry (note on
I, xiii, 8); for the past idea in *proxima* combined with the present
tense of *sum* cf. Virg. *Aen.* I, 198 *neque enim ignari sumus ante
malorum*.

   **5. sic te seruato possint gaudere parentes: me soror...
sentiat:** for this construction cf. the passage from Hor. *Od.* I,
xxviii quoted in the introduction above; also Hor. *Od.* I, iii, 1-9
*sic te diua potens Cypri...uentorumque regat pater...nauis, quae
tibi creditum debes Vergilium, finibus Atticis reddas incolumem
precor et serues animae dimidium meae*; and *CIL*, 1013 *si graue
non, hospes, fuerit, remorare, uiator: sic tibi sit felix quod pro-*

peratur iter; and Virg. *Ecl.* IX, 30–2 and X, 4–6. The speaker asks a favour of the person addressed and wishes him some good; the latter is to be a consequence of the former, or the former a condition of the latter.

7–8: presumably the family had heard that Gallus survived the fighting.

9. super: 'besides'; cf. Virg. *Aen.* VII, 461–2 *saeuit...ira super*, XI, 226–7 *ecce super maesti...legati responsa ferunt*, I, 29 *his accensa super...*.

[The text printed departs from that of the MS. tradition by reading[1] in line 6 *me soror Acca tuis sentiat e lacrimis* in place of *ne soror acta suis sentiat e lacrimis*. After mention of the other man's parents in line 5, *me* is almost inevitable before *soror* in line 6 to show whose *soror* is meant. There is then no room for the anyway awkward word *acta*, whereas the name of the sister is appropriate. For *Acca* as an Italian woman's name cf. Silius Ital. IX, 117. See also generally what is said in the introduction above. In line 5 the improbable though not wholly impossible *ut* of the MSS. has been excised, on the theory that it was inserted at some point to 'improve' a text already confused by corruption in line 6.]

XXII

1. qualis et unde genus, qui sint mihi, Tulle, Penates: Propertius answers all three questions by saying (3 and 9–10 below) that he comes from a particular part of Umbria; so there cannot be much difference in meaning between them. For *unde genus* cf. the Greek ποδαπός τὸ γένος (Aristophanes, *Peace* 186).

2. quaeris pro nostra semper amicitia: 'in virtue of our longstanding friendship'. *semper* cannot go with *quaeris*, for the thought of constant repetition of this simple question is ludicrous, though of course the question form is unreal (i.e. a 'figure') anyway. For the sense cf. I, xx, 1 *pro continuo amore*; and for the adjectival value of the adverb cf. Ter. *Andr.* 175 *eri semper lenitas*; cf. also above, I, iii, 44 and I, xvi, 47; and Cic. *Fin.* II, 84 *Puteolis granaria* = 'the grain-depots at Puteoli'.

---

[1] This reading, and the general interpretation of the poem that goes with it, was propounded in *Ut Pictura Poesis* (Festschrift Enk), Leyden 1955, by T. T. Sluiter, to whom any credit it may deserve is due. My own notes on this poem were written as they here stand without knowledge of Sluiter's article but subsequently to it.

3–10. si Perusina...: 'You know Perusia, grave of our countrymen who fell in the days of Italy's agony, when their own discord drove the Romans to their doom—and mine not least is the sorrow, o Tuscan earth; for on you, alas, my kinsman's bones were cast away, on you they lie, alas, unburied still. There I was born in fertile Umbria, where it borders on Perusia and lies below it in the plain.'

5. egit: cf. I, xiii, 28 and Hor. *Epod.* VII, 17 *sic est: acerba fata Romanos agunt*; Virg. *Aen.* IV, 465–6 *agit ipse furentem in somnis ferus Aeneas.* The translation depends on the context.

6. sed: a conjecture for *sit* of the MSS. It means 'but in particular...,' or 'yes, and in particular. ..'

7–8. Cf. the preceding poem.

9. campo is a quasi-instrumental ablative.

Propertius seems here to be saying that his birthplace was in the Umbrian plain, perhaps on a farm or an estate. At IV, i, 125 he mentions Asisium (on a hill above the plain) as honoured by his poetic success, and we can reasonably assume that this was his home-*town*. Perusia, on the hills across the plain from Asisium, was not an Umbrian but an Etruscan city: Propertius brings it into the present poem simply because it was a famous place, as Asisium at that time was not, and so a reference to it would afford a generally intelligible way of indicating the area in which he was born.

ADDENDA

III, 45. For *labi* said of 'falling' asleep, cf. Petronius XXI *cum laberemur in somnum*; XXII *cum Ascyttos laberetur in somnum*.

VI, 2 and 19. For the identity of the uncle see *C.R.* 5 (1955), 244–5.

VIII A, 7. *fulcire* here = 'tread'. It is found with the value 'press down' in Celsus VII, xix, 5, *linamenta* (the lint dressing, on a wound) *super non fulcienda sed leviter tantum imponenda sunt*; cf. also Persius I, 78, *Antiope aerumnis cor . . . fulta.* XI, 18.

IX, 23. According to another explanation, Love's action is like that of one who plays with a captive bird (Shaksp. *Romeo and Juliet*, II, ii, 177) or beetle (Aristoph. *Clouds* 762), keeping it on a string and now letting it fly a little, now checking it and pulling it back.

XI, 18. Another way of taking *timetur amor* in this passage is suggested by Ov. *Pont.* II, vii, 35–7 *non igitur uereor quo te rear esse uerendum, cuius amor nobis pignora mille dedit, sed quia res timida est omnis miser* etc. The wording of these lines, as of line 7 of the same poem—*da ueniam, quaeso, nimioque ignosce timori*—evidently contains echoes of our Propertian passage (lines 17–20 here); so that they acquire a special relevance to its interpretation. Ovid is writing from exile to a friend, and apologizing for asking to be reassured that the friend is still affectionate and loyal. It seems certain therefore that *non igitur uereor quo te rear esse uerendum* means 'not that I am anxious because I think that you are one *about whom* (i.e. about whose attitude) I need feel any anxiety. . . .' In which case in our Propertian passage *omnis timetur amor* may be expected to mean in effect 'any man is bound to feel nervous *about his beloved*' (literally: 'any love is object of anxiety').

9 780521 292108